Who Am I to Judge?

WHO AM I TO JUDGE?

Judicial Craft Versus Constitutional Theory

MARK TUSHNET

Yale

UNIVERSITY PRESS

NEW HAVEN & LONDON

Published with assistance from the foundation established in memory of Amasa Stone Mather of the Class of 1907, Yale College.

Yale University Press books may be purchased in quantity for educational, business, or promotional use. For information, please e-mail sales.press@yale.edu (U.S. office) or sales@yaleup.co.uk (U.K. office).

Set in Spectral type by Integrated Publishing Solutions.
Printed in the United States of America.

ISBN 978-0-300-27701-2 (paperback)
ISBN 978-0-300-27702-9 (hardcover)
Library of Congress Control Number: 2024937391
A catalogue record for this book is available from the British Library.

10 9 8 7 6 5 4 3 2 1

CONTENTS

Who Am I to Judge?

Introduction

In 2013, Pope Francis responded to a question about gays in the priesthood with five words, "Who am I to judge?" Many people's immediate response was puzzlement: Isn't that a big part of your job? The pope continued to defend his answer. His job wasn't to judge but to welcome, to comfort, to love, to show good will, and to guide.

Contrast that with the job description of a judge on the nation's highest court. The idea of judgment is baked into that description: Judges are supposed to, well, judge. Yet today we see something like a flight from judgment, and a reliance instead on constitutional theory. Justice Antonin Scalia disparaged the idea that judges should rest their decisions on "reasoned judgment," arguing that—at least in the abortion-related case he was dealing with—the term was simply a fig leaf for the personal predilections of the colleagues with whom he disagreed.

This book is a defense of reasoned judgment—or, in another formulation, of judging as a lawyer's craft—as against constitutional theory. It combines a historical examination of how Supreme Court justices have actually gone about interpreting the Constitution for most of the nation's history—an examination that shows that they typically didn't even have a constitutional theory in hand—with an inquiry into some fundamentals about why we have a constitution in the first place. In the past the justices offered us their reasoned judgments about the constitutional problems they were dealing with. Without pretending that the past was a golden era across the board, I argue that we can retrieve—and update—the idea of reasoned judgment and thereby improve our constitutional system. We should pay attention to judges' judgment, not their theories.

* * *

In the early 1980s, my friends Geof Stone and Mike Seidman asked me to join them in editing a new edition of a leading but outdated casebook on constitutional law. The first edition of our casebook was published in 1986 and was quite successful. Casebook publishers are close-mouthed about sales, but I think that for a while our book was the one most widely used in law schools. I think the reason for its success was that it caught the rising wave of interest in what this book calls constitutional theory. Almost simultaneously I wrote a series of articles critiquing prominent theories, which eventually led to my first book on constitutional theory, *Red, White, and Blue: A Critical Analysis of Constitutional Law* (1988). The book ended with the line, "Critique is all there is."

Having taken that position, I turned to topics other than constitutional theory—several books about Justice Thurgood Marshall, work on comparative constitutional law. I'm returning to constitutional theory now because the lesson that critique is all there is has been forgotten (or perhaps was never fully learned). From the early 2000s to today, constitutional theory has become a preoccupation of Supreme Court justices, legal scholars, and members of what political scientists call the "attentive public" who pay attention to what's going on in politics and especially the Supreme Court.

What's come back is the theory of originalism. Chapter 4 describes some recent attempts to address—and refute—originalism as a theory. My aim in this book is different. I want to challenge the very idea that we—Americans generally but judges too—

should *have* a constitutional theory at hand (or at least have at hand a theory of interpretation like originalism).

Chapter 1 is an informal empirical and historical examination of lists of justices widely regarded as great (and not-so-great), and an even more informal examination of the characteristics of the Courts led by Charles Evans Hughes in the 1930s, Earl Warren in the 1950s, and John Roberts today. I summarize the characteristics associated with greatness in justices and high quality in Courts as good judgment. Once the idea of good judgment is unpacked, though, I argue that it can help us think about the qualities we want presidents and senators to look for when they nominate and confirm judges to the federal bench. Chapter 2 continues this effort by looking at several decisions from the 1930s, a time when Supreme Court justices didn't think that they were deploying theories of constitutional interpretation.

Chapter 3 moves into the land of constitutional theory. It defines two kinds of constitutional theory. One is "cosmic," to use a term from the Reagan-appointed federal judge J. Harvie Wilkinson. Cosmic constitutional theory purports to offer answers to constitutional questions across the entire range of the Constitution. I argue that cosmic constitutional theory and associated theories of interpretation don't really help us—or judges—figure out what to do. The other kind of constitutional theory is local, so to speak—a theory of free expression that might have different foundations from a theory of constitutionally prohibited searches and seizures, for example. These theories can be even more local: a theory of commercial speech with different foundations from a theory of demonstrations on public streets. Sometimes these local theories hang together somewhat loosely but judges using them don't worry too much about whether the way they justify finding some regulation of demonstrations unconstitutional is the same way they justify finding a search unconstitutional.

Then in Chapter 4 I look at originalism in more detail and

argue that asking whether it's a good theory of interpretation is a mistake because we don't really want our judges to have the right theory of interpretation. Chapter 5 continues the argument by addressing the common but misguided observation that "it takes a theory to beat a theory," first through an informal intellectual history and then through an examination of how one theory of interpretation actually displaces another.

The book's argument has an empirical and a normative part, which creates some difficulties in exposition because the two parts should run parallel but must be presented in sequence. I've chosen to put the empirical part first, but in the course of laying it out I occasionally refer to elements of the normative argument that won't be presented in detail until later in the book. So, a shorthand guide here: We should look for judges who are likely to display good judgment in their rulings (the empirical argument) and we shouldn't care whether they have a good theory about how to interpret the Constitution as a whole—and maybe we should worry a bit if they think they have such a theory (the normative part).

I sometimes frame what I'm writing about in terms of what presidents should do when they look for a nominee, because that's a handy way to identify some interesting issues. It's a bit artificial, though, and probably the best overarching perspective you should bring to the book is your status as a citizen: Suppose you think that the Supreme Court these days is doing a pretty good job or a spectacularly bad one. Is there anything about the justices or the Court as a whole that helps you understand the *quality* of its performance? The core argument of the book is that what matters, for good or bad, is whether the justices are exercising good judgment.

CHAPTER 1

Looking for Good Judgment
in All the Right Places

Constitutional theory is in the air at Senate hearings on Supreme Court nominations. Senator Charles Grassley asked Amy Coney Barrett a "softball" question during the hearings on her nomination to the Supreme Court: What is originalism? She replied, "I interpret the Constitution as a law, and . . . and I understand it to have the meaning that it had at the time people ratified it. So that meaning doesn't change over time and it's not up to me to update it or infuse my own policy views into it." Senator Ben Sasse explained his vote against the next nominee, Ketanji Brown Jackson: "at every turn . . . she not only refused to claim originalism as her judicial philosophy, she refused to claim any judicial philosophy at all."

Senators Grassley and Sasse thought that they could best explain to the public their politically driven choices about who should sit on the Supreme Court by talking about judicial philosophy and originalism, which I'll call one kind of "grand" constitutional theory. They are politicians and I'm in no position to question their political calculations. What I can say, though, is that they're wrong in focusing on constitutional theory in picking Supreme Court justices. Instead they should focus on qualities such as intellectual curiosity and wide exposure to human experience, the foundation for good judgment. That in brief is this book's argument.

WHAT IS CONSTITUTIONAL THEORY?
AN INTRODUCTION

What's the point of a democratic constitution? Briefly, to create institutions of governance that over time do a pretty good job of making the society better off. "Better off" has two components, sometimes in tension. The democratic component is that we're better off when public policy tracks what most people think makes them better off—at least if their preferences are reasonably stable and policies consistent with them don't lead to social or economic disaster. The "constitutionalist" component (not a great term but it's the best we have) is that we're better off when our policies advance some fundamental human values and don't violate some basic human rights.

All well and good, but there's an obvious problem. We're going to disagree about what policies make us better off. Should tax rates be high so that we can pay for a strong social safety net? Should they be low so that people are encouraged to come up with new technologies that make our lives better? We're also going to disagree about what institutional arrangements are most likely to generate the policies that make us better off. Should we rely heavily on democratically elected legislatures to advance and protect basic human values—including both material well-being and human rights? How much authority should we give judges to supervise legislative choices to ensure that they don't violate fundamental human rights?

These kinds of disagreement underlie the flight to constitutional theory. The hope is that we can agree on a constitutional theory that will tell us how to resolve ordinary political disagreements: Don't adopt policies or institutional arrangements that are inconsistent with the original understanding of the Constitution's words (originalism), for example, or Don't adopt policies that undermine our ability to change our minds about the policies we think will make us better off (a "democracy-promoting" theory).

It would be great if we could do that. The problem is that we can't. Not that we can't develop constitutional theories that have real intellectual integrity—that reasonable people *could* accept. One difficulty is that elaborating such a theory makes it incredibly complicated, unsuitable as something that will help ordinary people think about how we should govern ourselves. A deeper difficulty is that at least so far we haven't been able to come up with a single theory that most of us can agree upon. Typically we adhere to a theory that generates the results we like—which is to say, we reproduce at the level of choosing a theory the very disagreements theory is supposed to overcome. And then there's what I think is the deepest difficulty. The disagreements reproduce themselves *within* each theory. Even if we were all originalists, for example, we'd find that originalism tells those who like some policy that it's compatible with originalism and tells those who don't like the policy that it's *in*compatible with originalism.

Is there an alternative to constitutional theory as a solution to the problems created by disagreement about policies and constitutional fundamentals? For decades the answer was obviously Yes. Law was the solution, law understood as something influenced but not determined by policy preferences, as incorporating aspects of each constitutional theory to the extent appropriate for the problem at hand, as deployed by judges for whom the ordinary "moves" lawyers make—distinguishing cases or generalizing them, for example—were the air they breathe. Sometimes I call this a pluralist constitutional theory, but a better term for it is judicial craft, as traditionally understood.

That, in sum, is the book's argument. The critique of constitutional theory comes in Chapters 3 and 4, the argument for taking judicial craft seriously in Chapters 5 and 6. First, though, I offer a historical approach to make plausible the craft argument.

WHO ARE SUPREME COURT JUSTICES (MOSTLY)?

Justice William Brennan reportedly described Richard Posner, who had been a law clerk for Brennan, as one of two real geniuses he'd known during his life (the other was William O. Douglas). Posner helped create the field of law and economics and was appointed to the federal appeals court by Ronald Reagan. Toward the end of his judicial career Posner became increasingly outspoken on many—probably too many—topics. In 2016 he described the qualifications of the justices then sitting on the Supreme Court: "I sometimes ask myself whether the nine current Supreme Court justices . . . are the nine best-qualified lawyers to be justices. Obviously not. Are they nine of the best 100? Obviously not. Nine of the best 1,000? I don't think so. Nine of the best 10,000? I'll give them that."

The political scientist Gautam Mukunda writes, "Most Presidents are, by definition, mediocre." The same is true of Supreme Court justices, much as people who pay attention to the Supreme Court would like to deny it (especially academics and journalists who regularly have to grapple with the justices' work and sometimes even meet them in social settings). Most justices are perfectly competent. They (or their law clerks—I'll say something about that later) write opinions that get the job done without making gross legal mistakes or inadvertently planting time bombs that will cause some legal disaster five or ten years down the road. But that's about the best we can say for them.

And a fair number of people who practice in specialized areas might say that things are actually worse than that. Patent lawyers, specialists in pension law, and probably tax lawyers hold their breaths when the Court takes up a case in their fields. They worry—often correctly—that the justices don't know how the provisions they're considering mesh with other provisions in a complex network where a mistake at one point ripples through the system and disrupts well-settled understandings. These days they worry that the justices will deploy in their cases some general approaches to interpreting statutes that may make sense in some contexts but not, they fear, in their specialized areas. And then someone like me swoops in and says—again correctly—that actually just about every case the Court decides should be understood to be "specialized" in the way patent law is. That's rather discouraging, and I put the possibility aside to focus on the more common view that most of the justices do a decent job.

Sometimes justices know that they fit in the middle of the list from best to worst. Here are some examples from the twentieth century.

- *Owen Roberts,* one of the justices who, lore has it, switched in time to save the nine justices from Court-packing in 1937. Felix Frankfurter reported that Roberts once expressed his self-understanding by saying, "Who am I to revile the good God that he did not make me a Marshall, a Taney, a Bradley, a Brandeis, or a Cardozo?"—a list that, as we'll see, has three candidates for "greats" among the justices.
- *Potter Stewart,* a Supreme Court justice for twenty-two years, longer than some of the justices who are regarded as great. Stewart wrote his share of decisions, some of them important. He had been a journalist and he liked to get off lines that might make it into the *New York Times* "quotation of the day" box, and he's probably most remembered for one of them: His test for whether some magazine or movie was "hard core" pornography was, "I know it when I see it." Stewart retired in 1981 and you'd be hard pressed to find a younger scholar of constitutional

law who has any impression whatever about Stewart's contribution to constitutional law beyond that quotation.[1]

- *Harry Blackmun*, who referred to himself as "Old Number Three," Richard Nixon's third choice for the seat he took on the Court. A truly modest and nice man, Blackmun was unprepared for the job, stumbled a bit in his first years, and eventually became a decent—that is, mediocre—justice.

Most justices are pretty much interchangeable with respect to their impact on the law. Donald Trump had a list of about twenty potential Supreme Court nominees. He had his reasons for choosing Neil Gorsuch, Brett Kavanaugh, and Amy Coney Barrett. Had he faced slightly different political constraints he might have chosen Raymond Kethledge, Amul Thapar, or Thomas Hardiman without significantly changing what he and his supporters wanted and got from the Supreme Court. Suppose, though, a president wants to find someone who would make extraordinary contributions to the law. Or, once a nominee has been chosen, suppose you as an ordinary citizen wanted to think about whether the nominee was likely to do so. This chapter examines some of the things the president or you might want to think about.

THINKING ABOUT WHAT MAKES A JUDGE GREAT: LOOKING TO HISTORY

Senators Grassley and Sasse offered a "top-down" or deductive approach to picking judges: Find the right constitutional theory

---

1. I searched the Harvard Library's on-line catalogue of books and articles for the keyword "potter stewart" published between 2000 and 2022, and came up with a handful of items, most dealing with Stewart's views about the First Amendment. (My favorite is Carlos A. Camargo, *Potter Stewart and the Definition of Anaphylaxis*, 129 J. ALLERGY & CLINICAL IMMUNOLOGY 753 (2012), which appropriates the "I know it when I see it" line for non-legal purposes.)

and look for judges who adhere to it. This chapter offers a "bottom-up" or inductive alternative: Look back to find great judges and figure out what made them great—and then look for the same things in today's nominees.

The bottom-up approach has two branches. First, individual nominees: What qualities have the Court's most distinguished members had? How do those qualities affect the job they have to do? Is there anything specific we should look for on those rare occasions when one chief justice replaces another? Second, the Court as a whole. What qualities do "strong" Courts have, compared with weaker ones? How do the qualities of individual justices mesh with those of others to strengthen or weaken the Court?

Nothing is certain, of course, but looking at the past can help us make some informed guesses about the future. We'll see that whether a potential Supreme Court justice has the "right" theory about how to interpret the Constitution, and indeed whether she or he has *any* such theory, has almost nothing to do with whether the nominee will turn out to be a great justice or help strengthen the Court as a whole.

PICKING A JUSTICE

How does and should a president pick one nominee out of Posner's pool of ten thousand top lawyers? The starting point has to be the observation that presidents choose under political constraints. Sometimes they have strong reasons to satisfy political constituencies important to them (if they're looking to be reelected) or their party. Barack Obama had such a reason in looking for a Hispanic-American justice when he had the opportunity to nominate a successor to David Souter. (For the record, before the 2008 election I predicted that Obama's first nominee would be Sonia Sotomayor.) Donald Trump had the same type of reason for coming up with a list of potential nominees satisfactory to the Federalist Society. Franklin Roosevelt nominated William O. Douglas because he believed that appointing a Westerner would strengthen his political position in the Senate and in the West. I could go on almost indefinitely: Almost every nominee has been chosen at least in part because doing so would give the president some political boost on net—that is, would get more support from some constituencies than it would lose from others.

The major—and perhaps the only—exception is Herbert Hoover's nomination of Benjamin Cardozo to replace Oliver Wendell Holmes in March 1932. Though in 1932 Hoover wasn't the hard-line reactionary he later became, he was at most a moderate Progressive, whereas Cardozo was clearly somewhat—and maybe more than somewhat—to Hoover's left. The attentive legal community, though, would have seen passing him over for some other more routine nominee as scandalous. (And even that consensus view of Cardozo's stature might be seen as a political constraint on Hoover's options.)

Most of the time, then, a president will ask, "Who out of the ten thousand potential nominees satisfies the political constraints I face?" And then, "Of those possibilities, which one's nomination is likely to give me the greatest political boost?" And only then, "Of *those,* which one is likely to go down in history as a great choice?" The Cardozo example suggests, though, that occasionally a president might approach the choice differently: "I really care about the Constitution—and to some extent about my legacy. I want to nominate someone who will turn out to be a truly great justice even if I take a political hit for making that choice (maybe the history books will say that making the nomination was my finest hour)."

Either way, the president's going to have to look for some things that characterize great justices—and hope to find nominees with those qualities among the pool of ten thousand.

WHAT HISTORY MIGHT TELL US

Looking to the past might help. We might identify great Supreme Court justices from years ago and see if we can find some characteristics that most of them share. But we can't populate the list with justices who have the characteristics that we think beforehand lead to greatness. Better to ask informed observers to come up with their lists of great justices without giving them much guidance about how they should define greatness.

Law librarian Fred Shapiro looked around and found quite a few such surveys. It's best to cut off the list of candidates for greatness at some point in the past to reduce the influence of contemporary politics on the rankings. Here's Shapiro's "top ten" list from 2003:

1. John Marshall
2. Oliver Wendell Holmes, Jr.
3. Earl Warren
4. Louis Brandeis
5. Hugo Black
6. William J. Brennan
7. Benjamin Cardozo
8. Felix Frankfurter
9. William O. Douglas
10. William H. Rehnquist

I found a few later lists, which have minor differences, and I have some quibbles with this one. Chief Justice Rehnquist was still in office when the survey was conducted and probably should be excluded because of the possibility of "recency bias," though I note that he does appear on a list Professor Cass Sunstein published in 2014 (and Douglas doesn't). The point of relying on surveys, though, is to avoid injecting the author's biases into the list.

So it makes sense to use this one, which in any event seems generally sensible.[2]

I could proceed with biographical sketches of each justice or with a table showing where each fits into some scheme. I do have such a table in my files but it's too complicated to reproduce here. Instead I'll summarize what seem to me—a subjective judgment, note—the most salient characteristics of the great Supreme Court justices.

• *Longevity and age.* Law professor William Ross's analysis of "the ratings game" led him to conclude, "The most striking common denominator among highly ranked justices . . . is longevity of service." Seven of the ten justices on the list were in the top quarter of justices in their length of service. Longevity isn't enough to guarantee greatness: James Moore Wayne and John McLean (no, not John McClane) served longer than five of the justices on the list, and no one's heard of them since they left the Court.

When it matters—when deciding who to nominate—a president of course can't use actual longevity as a selection criterion. The potential nominee's age and general good health might be decent proxies for *potential* longevity: The younger the nominee the greater the chance that she or he will actually be on the Court for a long time. Three justices on the list were in their forties when they were nominated: Marshall (forty-six), Douglas (forty-one),

---

2. Another list, of justices who have appeared on U.S. postage stamps: John Jay, John Marshall, Joseph Story, Oliver Wendell Holmes, Jr., Louis Brandeis, William Howard Taft, Charles Evans Hughes, Hugo Black, Felix Frankfurter, Earl Warren, William Brennan, Thurgood Marshall, Ruth Bader Ginsburg. The criteria for selecting judges to appear on postage stamps aren't precisely the same as "perceived greatness," but the lists overlap enough to provide some support for my decision to use Shapiro's list as the basis of my analysis.

and Rehnquist (forty-seven). Four were in their fifties: Brandeis (fifty-nine), Black (fifty-one), Brennan (fifty), and Frankfurter (fifty-six). Young-*ish*, then, and in good health.

- *Location in political time.* Age at nomination is something the president can control. An important strand in political science dealing with the development of the U.S. constitutional order emphasizes that we can see a succession of what I call political regimes. Each regime starts, stays on the scene for a while, and then fades—this pattern defines what the political scientist Stephen Skowronek famously called "political time." For the twentieth century there's the "New Deal/Great Society" regime and the "Reagan Revolution" regime. Each regime has some distinctive features, including a set of governing ideas and ideologies about the role of government in American life, the substantive values government should advance, and more. Presidents identify these ideas and ideologies in their campaign speeches, inaugural addresses, State of the Union speeches, and implicitly in their choices for the Supreme Court. That's because in each regime, Supreme Court opinions can be another place where these ideas and ideologies are articulated.

Where are the great justices located in political time? With few exceptions each came to the Supreme Court at a key moment in political time. John Marshall was appointed as ordinary politics kicked in after the dominating figure of George Washington left the scene. Louis Brandeis was an important voice for Progressive ideas about economic regulation even before his appointment to the Court. Black, Frankfurter, and Douglas were all major figures in the creation of the New Deal regime; William Rehnquist became chief justice as part of the Reagan Revolution. Earl Warren and William Brennan fit into political time a bit differently. Eisenhower appointees, they came to office when the New Deal order was consolidated through its acceptance by the mainstream

Republican party. Only Holmes and Cardozo were great even though they didn't come to the Court at a key moment in political time—and as we'll see they are distinctive in another way.

Some presidents shape their own location in political time, instituting a new regime like Roosevelt and Reagan or consolidating an established one like Eisenhower. Such presidents have the opportunity to shape the Supreme Court as well, which is to say that they have a chance to nominate a justice who will turn out to be great. Presidents who get a chance to nominate justices when a regime is running smoothly or, worse, when it's fading from the scene, don't really have that chance. That's going to matter when we return at the end of this chapter to thinking about nominating justices in the near future.

• *Prior experience in public life.* I began this project believing the Court in recent years had suffered because it didn't have many justices who had had significant and sustained experience in high executive or legislative office. The list of great justices doesn't confirm that particular guess. Instead, it shows that great justices have had significant experience in national public life in some capacity. Some were legislators (Marshall in the House of Representatives, Black in the Senate). Others served in important positions as political executives (Marshall as secretary of state, Warren as governor and presidential candidate, Douglas as chair of the Securities and Exchange Commission, and Rehnquist as assistant attorney general).[3] Frankfurter and Brandeis were important public intellectuals. And Marshall and Holmes had military experience that decisively shaped the way they understood political life.

---

3. I have some questions about describing Rehnquist's position as an "important" one relative to the experience of others but, as I discuss below, nothing really turns on how those questions are answered.

I turn now to one negative point and one positive point about the great justices.

- *NOT A JUDGE.* I put this in capital letters because it's common today to think that justices have to have been judges. Not the great ones. True, there are three people on the list whose major work experience before coming the Court was as a judge. Two were truly exceptional cases, though. Both Holmes and Cardozo were *the* judges for the era before they were appointed. Holmes had written a classic book about the common law and published a large number of great articles, some of which are close to being required reading even today for people who want to become literate in the law. Cardozo had delivered lectures about jurisprudence and legal method that both captured and shaped thinking about those topics. The only equivalent to Holmes and Cardozo in the modern period is Richard Posner. I know of no sitting judge today anywhere near the stature of those three.

  That leaves William Brennan. The conclusion I draw is that hoping that someone whose primary work experience is judging will turn out to be a great justice is a bet with low odds of a payoff. Appellate judges make competent—mediocre, again—justices but not more.

- *Intellectual curiosity.* According to Gautam Mukunda, academics who study leadership in all sorts of organizations have concluded that what they call intellectual brilliance matters. But, he observes, "brilliance" might not be precisely the right word. It's not that successful leaders are off-the-charts smart as measured by standard intelligence tests, but rather that they are intellectually curious: They see something new and want to find out about it; they wonder why something isn't working well in their organization or at the airport and look for clues in unusual places like science fiction.

  It's obviously difficult to measure intellectual curiosity from the outside, and anything one says about whether another person has it will inevitably have a significant subjective component. That said, we can look for behaviors that might correlate with intellectual curiosity.

And when I look at the list of great justices, the fact that all but two had intellectual curiosity in spades jumps off the page. (The exceptions are Earl Warren and William Brennan.) John Marshall wrote a well-regarded biography of George Washington that's also a general history of late eighteenth-century America. William Rehnquist wrote several books about constitutional history. We know that Oliver Wendell Holmes read extraordinarily widely, although he shunned dry social science, and that Louis Brandeis relished reading the books that Holmes disdained. Cardozo was well read in psychology and social science. Hugo Black's library is filled with classics of political theory containing his own annotations. Felix Frankfurter stuck his nose into almost everything political and hung out and tried to keep up with novelists and some artists. William O. Douglas was a devoted environmentalist and internationalist who wrote books describing the natural world and life in the nations he visited. It's not that they would have been *good* novelists or ecological scientists or sociologists, but that they were interested in novels and ecology and science.[4]

When a president interviews the people being considered for a nomination to the Supreme Court, some questions that ought to be on the list might be "What was the most interesting novel you read recently? What's your favorite novel? What movies have you enjoyed seeing over the past couple of years? What's your favorite movie?" along with or maybe even instead of the anodyne

---

4. I might be wrong in describing Brandeis and Black as intellectually curious. Each might have read outside the law for instrumental purposes: Black for self-improvement, and Brandeis to enhance his ability to pursue effective public interest litigation. I'm inclined to think that the reasons for reading outside the law don't matter much.

"What's your judicial philosophy? How do you think the Constitution should be interpreted?," which will elicit from reasonably sophisticated candidates entirely predictable and unilluminating answers. Potential nominees will be able to game the alternative questions a bit—a canned answer about some classic book or movie, for example—but sticking in "recent" might give them enough pause to elicit genuine answers.

Running a Little Law Firm

Having been a senior partner at a large law firm, Justice Lewis Powell knew what he was talking about when he described the Court as a group of "nine little law firms." Each justice has to manage her or his office, and only some have had managerial experience before coming to the Court. Solicitors-General manage small offices (Elena Kagan, Thurgood Marshall); law school deans manage larger ones (Elena Kagan again, Harlan Fiske Stone). Justices regularly say that it takes about five years to settle in to the Court. One reason is that each justice has to develop a managerial style that gets the "law firm's" work done as well as it can.

Management has nothing to do with having a judicial philosophy—indeed having a judicial philosophy might interfere with a judge's ability to run her office well—but management does have something to do with practicing law and so isn't entirely unrelated to the craft of judging.

For the public the most important part of a judge's work is of course the opinions coming from the office (or "chambers," as they're called in Court-speak). Shortly after she completed her clerkship with Justice Clarence Thomas, Laura Ingraham told television viewers that she had drafted opinions for the justice, sent them in to his office, and got them returned basically rewritten from top to bottom. I was on the same program, to talk about what it was like to clerk for Justice Thurgood Marshall. When

Ingraham described her work, my immediate reaction—though I didn't express it—was, "If I were a justice and had to do that, I'd fire the law clerk."

In Justice Marshall's chambers the law clerks did opinion-drafting, as law clerks have done in almost every chambers since sometime in the 1960s—with revealing exceptions. In Justice Marshall's chambers, one clerk would draft an opinion, and the two other clerks would go over it in great detail, criticizing both its arguments and the way they were presented.[5] By the time an opinion eventually went to the justice, it was quite polished. He would have been really angry with us if he had to tear it apart and rebuild it from the ground up. We sometimes did send him drafts he didn't like. He let us know his views by hanging on to the opinions instead of sending them back to us with some minor editorial changes. After waiting a couple of weeks to hear from him, we'd figure out that he didn't like the draft, go into his office and take it back, and start over. That was *his* managerial style, and I think, though of course I'm biased, that it was a pretty good way to get well-crafted opinions out of the chambers.

I don't question Ingraham's description but now have a more generous view. The key is that Ingraham clerked for Justice Thomas in his second year on the Court. He had been a manager as chair of the Equal Employment Opportunity Commission, and in that capacity he probably reviewed material produced for him by his staff—speeches, but also legal analyses to accompany his opinions as a commissioner. I don't know what his managerial style was at the EEOC; for obvious reasons people who write about him don't focus on such a minor feature of his background. But, whatever his style was, the work of the Court is different

5. Today each justice is authorized to hire four law clerks, the chief justice five (and retired justices can hire one law clerk who sometimes is "assigned" by the retired justice to another chambers).

enough that justices have to develop managerial styles appropriate to *that* work. And doing so takes time.

For one thing, justices have to figure out how to hire law clerks who can reliably produce the kind of drafts they want to see. Early on, justices can't really be sure that they have assembled the kind of office they want. And, feeling some psychological pressure to "do their own work," early on justices do more opinion-drafting than they will five and ten years later. As economists would put it, they learn that the marginal contribution they make to what law clerks produce in a well-managed office isn't worth their personal effort. They find out that they have better things to do than worry through the details of some complicated provisions of the nation's bankruptcy or pension laws, and leave that to their law clerks.

They find out as well that as they age they have less intellectual energy to devote to work that they found easy when they were younger. The law clerks' role in drafting has grown substantially since the 1960s, but we have enough papers from justices who served during the 1960s and 1970s to be able to say with some confidence that justices do more drafting of opinions in their early years on the Court than they do later, when they give their law clerks more drafting responsibility.

Justices also want their opinions to sound like them—or, in the current way of putting it, they want to develop a distinctive voice. Early on there's just not enough material for a law clerk to work with to capture the justice's voice. After about five years, though, the pile of opinions from the justice's chambers has grown, and like good speechwriters, the law clerks can reproduce the justice's voice.[6]

---

6. I've heard that sometimes aspiring law clerks "prep" for their interviews with justices who are considering hiring them by reviewing a large number of the justice's published opinions. That exercise means that the clerks who do

Today's justices keep up the pretense that they write their own opinions, through a trope they'll all offer if pressed. What's their process for producing opinions? They talk with their law clerks about the case and identify the major points the opinion should cover. You can do that either in conversation, as Justice Marshall did, or on paper, as Justice Ginsburg said she did. One law clerk is assigned the job of producing a draft, and—in well-organized chambers, at least—the other clerks vet the draft before sending it to the justice. And here's where the trope comes in: Justices say they do a "heavy edit" of the draft.

We won't be sure until the papers from some modern chambers become available, but I'm skeptical about the adjective "heavy." As I've said, once the justice has figured out how to hire a group of clerks that fits his or her style of judging, the draft opinions should be in pretty good shape. Justice Sotomayor pointed out that sometimes she might not have brought up some specific point important to one or another justice in her discussions with her law clerks—an inadvertent oversight that will indeed require some editing, and it's probably more efficient for the justice to insert the appropriate discussion than to tell the law clerk what the problem is and have the law clerk do it.

The justice will probably add something to the opinion or take something out: Justice Ginsburg probably inserted the words "path-marking" in places where the law clerks hadn't (and might have taken the words out where the law clerks had inserted them). Other justices might come up with a line or two that they think captures their thinking particularly well. And, when the opinions really matter to the justice because they deal with an issue close to her or his heart, the justice will write paragraphs rather than

---

get hired will already have some sense of the justice's voice. Because I'm relying in part on my experience of clerking for Justice Marshall, I note that I didn't do anything like that before my interview with him.

lines—and again, drop them into the opinion. Not infrequently this doesn't produce seamless opinions, and careful readers can make some guesses about where the law clerk's language ends and the justice's begins.

Reasonable people can disagree about whether the process I've described should be called "heavy" editing. I personally would drop the adjective. I admit too that the more seemingly critical observations I've made are speculation—informed speculation, I think, but still speculation. Two additional speculations: Justices say they heavily edit their clerks' draft for reasons of self-esteem. To say otherwise would be to hint at the possibility that a lot of other people could do just as good a job as the justice. And law clerks will rush to their justices' defense, confirming that even though Ingraham's description of her work doesn't really describe their own, the justice they worked for really did heavily edit their drafts.

I end with two stories, one about an appendix to an opinion and the other about a footnote, that illustrate how justices use their law clerks sensibly even if the clerks end up committing their justice to a mistake. They are speculative reconstructions, but I'm reasonably confident that the broad outlines are accurate.

The *Dobbs* decision overturning *Roe v. Wade* relied heavily on an account of the status of abortion in the laws of the United States before 1868, when the Fourteenth Amendment was adopted. Justice Alito's opinion contained an appendix supporting the proposition that "the vast majority of States enacted statutes criminalizing abortion at all stages of pregnancy" by listing those states. "All stages of pregnancy" mattered because *Roe* and its defenders asserted that historically abortion had been permitted before "quickening." If that were so, Justice Alito's argument would have been weakened, and indeed one might begin to construct an argument that traditionally the right to obtain an abortion before quickening was constitutionally protected. The opinion vouched for the list's accuracy by saying in a footnote that an amicus brief "incorrectly exclude[d] two states" from its parallel list.

How was the list in the appendix compiled? Probably by consulting a book and a law review article, both by pro-life activists, featured in amicus briefs filed on behalf of the author of one of those works and by two prominent pro-life legal academics, and then cited in the opinion. Justice Alito probably told his law clerks to pull from the works the list he wanted and to organize them chronologically rather than alphabetically, as was done in the law review article. He then probably reviewed the list the law clerk developed, either by looking at copies of the statutes supplied by the law clerk or by clicking through links to the statutes in some electronic data base.

So far, so good. Here's the problem. The list includes an Alabama statute enacted in 1841 making it a crime to "willfully administer *to any pregnant woman* any medical, drugs, . . . or any thing whatever . . . with the intent to procure the miscarriage of such woman." Justice Alito (or his law clerk) put the italics there to show that the statute did indeed prohibit abortion at any stage of pregnancy. The problem is that in 1857 Alabama's Supreme Court interpreted the statute to prohibit only post-quickening abortions.

The mistake isn't a big deal, and correcting it certainly wouldn't have changed the outcome. It does suggest, though, that a justice's entirely sensible decision to run his office by relying on law clerks for such tedious chores can sometimes misfire.

Yates v. United States involves another list. The case involved a statute making it a crime for someone to destroy "tangible objects" to "impede a federal investigation." The issue before the Court was whether a fish was a tangible object. The case facts make it a wonderful teaching tool—undersized red snappers, a law generated by the Enron scandal, and more—but recounting them would take too much space and time. The Court held that a fish wasn't a tangible object within the statute's meaning. Justice Kagan dissented. Her opinion referred to the Dr. Seuss book *One Fish, Two Fish, Red Fish, Blue Fish*—probably inserted by the justice herself—to support the proposition that "[a] fish is . . . a discrete thing that possesses a physical form." (I detect a seam here between what the law clerk's draft said and what the justice wrote herself.)

Justice Kagan's central point was that *of course* a fish was a tangible object if the words had their ordinary meaning. "Dozens of federal laws . . . (and hundreds of state enactments) include the term 'tangible object [or thing]'" and none of them, she wrote, had "[t]o [her] knowledge" been interpreted as narrowly as the majority did in this case. And here's the footnote: "From Alabama and Alaska through Wisconsin and Wyoming (and trust me—in all that come between), States similarly use the terms." The implicit list here was probably generated in the way the list in *Dobbs* was. Justice Kagan probably told her law clerk to go through the statute books of every state (electronically, probably) to find statutes using the terms, and then give her a memo listing them all (and maybe asking for hard copies of the statutes). She then probably checked the list for accuracy, either by reading each of the cited statutes or—more reasonably—by spot-checking the memo, reading a handful of randomly chosen statutes or links.

When she wrote "trust me," she was asking us to trust her that she had hired trust-worthy law clerks and then figured out a sensible way to supervise their work—and there's nothing wrong with that even if it someday turns out that Pennsylvania or one of the other states that "come between" had actually interpreted the statute's term more narrowly than she would, though less narrowly than the majority had.

The lessons? First, justices have to figure out how they should spend their own time and what sorts of things they can use their law clerks for. Only a bad manager or an inexperienced justice would try to compile the lists in *Dobbs* and *Yates* himself or herself. Most justices appear to have decided that letting their law clerks produce initial drafts and then editing the drafts "heavily" or otherwise is the best use of the *justice's* time. I have no reason to question that managerial decision.

Second, however: Trust most of the time but verify if you care a lot about details.

I stress that I don't regard my speculative comments—note all the "probablys"—as criticisms of the justices. I think that the practices I've described and speculated about demonstrate that justices develop managerial styles that fit their personalities and understandings of their role *and* lead them to send out from their chambers the best that the justice can do. And, again, these matters of managerial style have a lot to do with getting good judicial work done and nothing to do with constitutional theory.

Maybe it's superfluous to return to this chapter's overarching themes about choosing justices, but here goes. Even though a justice does manage a little law firm, we shouldn't worry about whether a nominee has enough managerial experience. She'll develop that experience soon enough and isn't likely to do much damage in the meantime. But, as each justice's chambers comes to resemble a little law firm producing collaborative work, the chances are that the work will "regress to the mean," that is, tend to become mediocre. The bureaucratization of the Court, therefore, might limit the possibility of judicial greatness emerging in the future.

PICKING A COURT

When we pick a new Supreme Court justice we're also adjusting the assets in our portfolio. Unlike the manager of financial assets, though, we can neither replace underperforming assets whenever we want, nor add new assets that might synergistically improve the portfolio's performance.[7] Justices have to retire before we can look at the Court as a whole. And, as ever, political constraints might mean that a president would face high costs in trying to re-jigger the assets to make the Court as a whole "better" from some not entirely political point of view.

We can still learn something about picking justices from looking at the Court as a whole. I have to face some problems of method up front, though. *What* "Court as a whole" should we look at? Conventionally we talk about "the Hughes Court," "the Warren Court," and the like. As scholars have known for quite a while, differentiating Courts by the simple label of their chief justices is entirely arbitrary. We know, for example, that there were at least two Warren Courts, one running from Earl Warren's appointment through Felix Frankfurter's retirement, the other from then to Warren's retirement—and, with the major exception of the first Warren Court's work on segregation, only the second one is the activist Warren Court.

We have surveys of great Supreme Court justices to help us think about picking a single justice. I don't know of similar surveys of "Courts as a whole." So, I have to rely on my subjective assessment of Court performance to develop a "theory" of the Court-as-portfolio. And my ability to do that is limited by the degree to which I'm familiar with the Court's work during any particular time period. I have no clue, for example, about whether to rate as "strong" or "weak" the Court from 1903 to 1910 if that turned out to be a sensible time period for assessing the Court as a whole.

Here's what I did: I began with my subjective sense that the

7. For synergy to be possible we have to think of some of the portfolio's assets as material capital rather than stocks and bonds, but there's no reason not to do so.

Court during the 1930s was pretty strong, as was the Court during Earl Warren's chief justiceship, and that the Court under Warren Burger was noticeably weaker. Then, to avoid the arbitrariness of the "Chief Justice" periodization, I looked for what political scientists call "natural courts" during those periods. Natural courts are courts whose membership is stable—no one leaves, so no one new comes in. Conveniently, there are natural courts from March 14, 1932, to August 18, 1937 (during Hughes's tenure), from October 14, 1958, to March 24, 1962 (during Warren's), and from December 19, 1975, to September 24, 1981 (Burger's). Equally conveniently, these natural courts lasted long enough for me to be able to assign, again subjectively, an evaluation of the work of those "Courts as a whole." And, probably most convenient, the natural Court in the late 1950s to early 1960s seems to me intermediate in strength between the other two.

What do these natural courts look like? Here I examine the composition of certain natural courts and categorize their justices according to one of the characteristics I used in discussing individual justices—the primary legal experience each justice had before appointment (Table 1).

I must note immediately that this interpretation is shot through with subjective judgments. I've put Warren Burger and William Rehnquist in the category for "some public service" because each was an assistant attorney general in the federal Department of Justice but not attorney general (as McReynolds, Stone, and Clark were) or deputy attorney general (White). Maybe, though, they should be shifted to the "substantial public service—executive" box. It seems a bit odd to treat Louis Brandeis's and Thurgood Marshall's work as public interest lawyers as mere private practice like Pierce Butler's. Maybe they should be shifted into the "some public service" box. Potter Stewart served briefly on the Cincinnati city council; that's some elected public service, though I wouldn't want to call it substantial. As it happens, the

Table 1. Legal Experience of Justices, in "Natural Courts" of the Past

Natural court	Substantial public service—elected	Substantial public service—executive branch	Judicial	Some public service	Private practice
Hughes period	Sutherland Hughes	McReynolds Stone	Van Devanter Hughes Cardozo	Van Devanter	Brandeis Butler Roberts
Warren period	Black Warren	Douglas Clark	Brennan Harlan Whittaker Stewart	Frankfurter	Harlan
Burger period	NONE	White Marshall	Brennan Stewart Burger Blackmun Stevens	Burger Rehnquist Powell	Marshall Powell

most interesting conclusions to be drawn from comparing this grouping to one using the same categories for the Court today wouldn't change if we made all of those moves.

If we make similar categorizations for the justices on the Court today, three things jump out (Table 2):

- The disappearance of justices with substantial experience in elected office—such as that of two governors of major states in the earlier comparison (Hughes for New York, Warren for California) who also ran for president.
- The disappearance of justices whose primary legal experience was in private practice.
- The increasing number of justices whose primary legal experience was as a judge.

Recall that, in my view, the strength of the Court as a whole diminished from the Hughes natural Court through the Warren and Burger ones. This suggests to me at least that we could get better Courts if our portfolio had one or two people with substantial experience in elected office, one or two from private practice (including the liberal or conservative public interest bar), and a smaller number of judges.

In light of today's partisan polarization the idea of choosing elected politicians for the Court will probably send shivers up the spine. People will ask: "How can a *politician* think about legal issues with only the law and not politics in mind?" I've devoted a lot of my academic career to arguing that the distinction between law and politics doesn't exist. I believe that many academics, including a decent number of conservatives, would agree that the distinction is overdrawn even if they disagree with my stronger claim that the distinction between law and politics is illusory.

I'll illustrate this with some examples, with the qualification that any name I mention will become outdated even between the

Table 2. Legal Experience of Justices, the Supreme Court Today

	Substantial public service—elected	Substantial public service—executive branch	Judicial	Some public service	Private practice
Today's court	NONE	Thomas Kagan	Roberts Thomas Alito Sotomayor Gorsuch Kavanaugh Barrett Jackson	Roberts Alito Gorsuch Kavanaugh Jackson	NONE

time I send this to press for publication and the day it's available to readers.

Donald Trump's lists of possible nominees ended up with four Republican senators: Tom Cotton, Ted Cruz, Josh Hawley, and Mike Lee. The first three were probably just for show: Each has ambitions to be president. Mike Lee, though, was a plausible conservative nominee. For Democrats the most obvious name was until recently Representative Jamie Raskin. Other possibilities might be Senator Amy Klobuchar and Vice President Kamala Harris.

When, relying on the kind of analysis I've just gone through, I floated Representative Raskin's name on social media, I got the immediate push-back, "He's *too old*."[8] In 2023 Raskin was sixty-one years old (Klobuchar was sixty-three, Harris fifty-eight). When they were nominated as chief justices, Hughes was sixty-seven and Warren sixty-two. One of the constraints contemporary presidents face in choosing nominees is indeed age. The U.S. system of life tenure means that a president can effectively "pack" the Court by choosing younger nominees who will be around for a long time: Clarence Thomas (forty-three when nominated), Brett Kavanaugh (forty-three), Amy Coney Barrett (forty-eight). The push for relatively youthful nominees fits badly with the possibility that someone could have "substantial" public service in elected office.

The same problem probably attends finding a nominee from private practice. Trump's list did have Paul Clement on it. After serving as solicitor general, Clement became a leading member of the Supreme Court bar, regularly arguing cases for private and public interest clients before the Court. By 2025 Clement will be fifty-seven years old, probably on the wrong side of the "too old"

8. Representative Raskin's cancer diagnosis would of course count against his nomination no matter what his age.

line. On the progressive side there's no one who dominates in the way Louis Brandeis and Thurgood Marshall did, but perhaps a Democratic president could find an unexpected—and relatively young—public interest lawyer to nominate.

I suspect, though, that our political polarization means that we'll continue to pick too many judges to be justices.

The Special Problem (?) of the Chief Justice

Now switch the metaphor about the Court as a whole from a portfolio to a team. Teams exist to get things done—widgets made, reports published, whatever. Effective teams ordinarily have leaders. The leader tells team members what subtasks to do: write one section of the report, find good illustrations, design the layout. Leaders make these decisions based upon their evaluation of the team members' different abilities.

The most important thing to know about the chief justice of the Supreme Court is that he (so far only he) can't possibly be that kind of leader. John Roberts said that as chief justice he wanted to make the Court more collegial, more cooperative in reaching results, with fewer divisions in the outcomes even in controversial cases, and less contentious verbal confrontations between the justices in their opinions. References to the need for the chief justice to build consensus pervaded his confirmation hearings. All that was probably just for show, perhaps including even Roberts's own posturing.

The reason is that the chief justice doesn't have any of the tools that other leaders of real teams have. He can't fire someone who doesn't do what the chief justice wants—even one who doesn't do much at all. He can't discipline a colleague who calls other justices names in writing. Indeed, my reading of justices' papers from the 1960s and 1970s leads me to conclude to no one even asks—at least in writing—that a colleague dial the tone of an opinion back a bit.

A chief justice can't set and enforce ethical standards for his judicial colleagues. Chief Justice Roberts presided over a Court where norms of civility broke down so severely that someone leaked a full draft opinion—not merely the results in a pending case, which hasn't been all that rare in the Court's history—and then investigators couldn't even find out who the leaker was.

The chief justice can tell colleagues which opinions they should write if they're both in the majority. You might imagine that this power could be used as a modest tool to keep colleagues in line. The chief justice could communicate (discreetly and without being explicit), "Behave and I'll give you good opinions to write; misbehave and I'll give you the dogs" (that being the jargon in the Court for deadly boring cases involving highly technical matters—these days involving bankruptcy, pension, and tax law). Or the reverse: Responding to an effusive introduction Justice Kagan gave him, Chief Justice Roberts joked that people wouldn't be reading pension law opinions by her for a while. That's possible but even that power is quite limited. The justices have developed a strong internal norm that by the end of the year each one should have written roughly the same number of majority opinions. So, if the Court decides eighty-one cases in one term, each justice should write nine majority opinions, plus or minus one or two. A chief justice constrained by the norm doesn't have a free hand in doling out the good cases and the dogs.

Even more, each justice has an obvious strategy for avoiding the dogs. The chief justice can assign opinions only to those who are with him in the majority. You can escape getting a dog by dissenting. You don't even have to write a dissent: You might simply write, "I dissent because of the reasons powerfully developed by Judge A in the lower court." Or, even more subtly, you can dissent before opinions are assigned, then say that the opinion—by someone else—has persuaded you to withdraw your dissenting vote.

The Court understood as a team does have to get things done. In one of the few really useful studies offering an analytic take on the chief justice's work, the political scientist David Danelski says that like all teams the Court needs a "task leader" and a "social leader." Somebody has to run the Conference—the meetings of the justices after they've heard oral arguments where they discuss the cases and cast their tentative votes. By tradition and by default the chief justice runs it. Each chief justice brings his managerial style to the Conference. Chief Justice Hughes ran the Conference with an iron hand. He had a prodigious memory and a powerful legal mind. He would spend many minutes presenting a case's facts in detail and outlining the arguments on both sides. That had the effect of preempting discussion by his colleagues. Reacting to his experience with Hughes as Conference leader, his successor, Harlan Fiske Stone, let discussions wander wherever his colleagues wanted to go—another way of managing badly. The reverse problem occurred with Warren Burger, who like Stone couldn't manage the Conference, in part because Burger wasn't nearly as good a legal analyst as were many (most? all?) of his colleagues. Burger's replacement by William Rehnquist was greeted with a sigh of relief from the other justices; William Brennan ranked Rehnquist above Earl Warren and of course above Burger as the best chief justice with whom he served.

This history suggests that the chief justice *shouldn't* always be the task leader at the Conference. William Howard Taft relied on Willis Van Devanter so much that Justice Brandeis wrote in 1922 that Van Devanter "runs the Court now." Earl Warren and William Brennan met before the Conference to map out what would happen there, and after it to hash out opinion assignments. There's a sense in which Warren and Brennan shared the job of Conference leader. The jobs Danelski identifies do have to be done but they don't have to be done by the chief justice—and sometimes they'd be done better by someone else.

Only a handful of presidents have an opportunity to nominate a chief justice. Those who get the chance shouldn't think that picking a chief justice is much different from choosing an associate justice, because what the chief justice can do is not much more than what an associate justice can do.

WHAT MAKES A GOOD JUSTICE?

Putting things together: What markers help us make a decent guess about the possibility that a person about to be nominated for the Supreme Court will turn out to be better than mediocre? Answer: intellectual curiosity, and substantial experience in public life as something other than a judge.

For greatness we have to ask, Where are we in political time? Along with others I believe we are near an inflection point, with some new political regime around the corner—either progressive Democratic or MAGA Republican. If the former, Justice Ketanji Brown Jackson might be well positioned to become a great justice; if the latter, Justice Amy Coney Barrett.[9] Except for the "not a judge" marker. Maybe, though, we should reconsider that description.

Why do intellectual curiosity and substantial experience in public life help us make decent guesses about the future? Because people with those characteristics have had wide contact with people in many spheres of life, either imaginatively or in person. They have seen people at their best and sometimes at their worst.

It's not that a person serving as attorney general has those contacts daily. Rather, it's that they have done things to get in that position that gave them such contacts. William Rehnquist was an on-the-ground Republican activist in Arizona, for example, and in that capacity he had to have interacted with all sorts of people.

9. I suspect that many readers will disagree with my sense that Justice Barrett's association with the People of Praise, an association of conservative Catholics, is a "plus" in the "life experience" column.

Notably, working as an appellate lawyer in a high-powered law firm doesn't give you *those* kinds of contacts, and neither does working in the White House counsel's office or as a legal functionary in the Department of Justice (though it gives you other contacts useful in getting a job as a federal judge).

Seeing things in this light might lead us to modify the "not a judge" marker. Trial court judges, especially trial court judges in state courts, do have the kind of contact with people in all phases of their lives that senators and governors and people deeply shaped by their military experience have. That might bring Justice Brown Jackson back into contention, especially if we treat her relatively brief time as a public defender as relevant.

Finally, and most important, why does wide contact matter? Because, I believe, it is the best way of learning both what good judgment is and how to exercise it. You see people facing all sorts of problems and doing something about them, you think hard about whether they made good or bad choices, and sometimes you have to make similar choices yourself. Wide contact with all sorts of people is something like an inoculation against constitutional theory. Or maybe it's enough to say that wide contact makes it easier for a judge to exercise reasoned judgment.

CHAPTER 2

Judging Without Theory
The 1930s

As I suggested in the Introduction, constitutional theory is a relatively recent development, dating from the last quarter of the twentieth century. We might be able to see what judging without a theory looks like by looking at opinions written before then. I've chosen to use some cases from the 1930s as my vehicle, because I spent more than a decade working on a book about the Court during the 1930s and became far more familiar with the decisions and the justices from that period than I am with those of any other. Cases both obscure and prominent show the Court's most talented justices deciding cases—what judging without theory actually looks like. That will give us a decent sense of what exercising "reasoned" or good judgment is.

Some words of warning: Understanding why the opinions don't use constitutional theory will sometimes take us deep into the weeds. Alas, legal doctrines and their conceptual underpinnings aren't always as simple as we might hope—or as simple as op-ed writers make them in their 750-word columns. And three of the opinions we'll look at were written by Chief Justice Charles Evans Hughes. He was a brilliant lawyer, but no one today would call him an elegant stylist.

THE OBSCURE CASE OF *UNITED STATES V. WOOD*

In 1909 the population of the District of Columbia was about 325,000, of whom about 37,000 were employed by the federal government. The next twenty-five years saw the city grow to about 525,000 and federal employment to about 157,000, because of the expansion of the government during World War I and the early years of the New Deal. The city's growth had many effects, one of the least important of which was that it became difficult to put together juries to hear federal criminal cases. The reason: In 1909 the Supreme Court held that employees of the federal government (and people receiving pensions from it, including the remaining Civil War veterans) couldn't serve as jurors. Husbands couldn't serve on juries when their wives were on trial because the risk that they'd be biased was too high. Similarly when an employee was called to serve in a case against his (at the time) employer: The employee might vote in favor of the employer from fear of losing his job. In criminal cases the government—the prosecution—was pitted against an ordinary citizen, and the Court in 1909 held that the usual rule barring an employee from serving on a jury in cases involving his employer applied to government workers. The Court didn't deal with a constitutional issue in 1909. It was exercising its power as a policy-maker to set the rules for conducting federal criminal trials.

In 1909 that rule automatically disqualified only about 16 percent of the population eligible for jury service. By the 1930s it disqualified a significantly larger proportion: according to the government, around 44 percent.[1] Congress addressed the issue in

---

1. I came up with the figure of 16 percent after doing some messy calculations and I don't claim great precision for it. (Readers interested in the details should contact me.) Even if it's off by 10 percentage points the disparity would still be substantial—26 as against 44 percent, or roughly one quarter as against one half.

a statute in 1935, removing the automatic rule: Federal employees could be disqualified only if they had an actual bias either for or against the government. That changed the judge-made disqualification rule but raised a new question: Was a jury with federal employees on it a proper "jury" within the meaning of the Sixth Amendment guarantee of trial by jury?

United States v. Wood was a routine shoplifting case, a federal crime because it occurred in the District of Columbia. Federal employees had sat on Wood's jury and convicted him. He appealed to the Supreme Court, arguing that he hadn't received a fair trial as required by the Constitution. The Court rejected his claim.

Chief Justice Hughes's opinion had two parts. The first questioned the policy basis for the 1909 decision; the second held that no matter what the justices might think good policy was, the 1935 statute displacing the judge-made rule was constitutionally permissible. The first part reviewed the history of disqualification of employees from England before the Constitution was adopted and from the states in the early years of the republic. The opinion quoted early legal commentators who explained that the king's employees weren't automatically disqualified because much of what most of them did was quite remote from the criminal cases they were supposed to determine, and disqualification "might operate as a serious obstruction to justice."

Wood's lawyer found a statement from William Blackstone, whose treatise was hugely influential in the founding era, asserting a rule of automatic disqualification. But, Hughes wrote, "the point is pressed too far." Blackstone did list employment as one of the grounds for disqualification, along with "kin to either party" and "of the same society or corporation" with a party. For Hughes, this wasn't enough: Blackstone "did not refer specifically" to *government* employees in criminal cases. Hughes questioned the 1909 decision as well. "The Court was not aided by a careful or comprehensive presentation of the English precedents," and the Court couldn't "accept the ruling" from 1909 as "determinative."

Then he turned to the 1935 statute and the Constitution. The Sixth Amendment guaranteed "trial by jury." The Court had to interpret those words: What are "the essential elements" of a trial by jury? Relying on a recent decision involving a trial where the defendant agreed to sending the case to a jury of eleven when one juror became ill, Hughes said that the essential elements were "twelve men," a judge with the power to instruct them, and unanimous verdicts. "None of these elements was involved here." We'll see Hughes making this kind of move again: taking a statement that's clearly shaped by the facts of the case at hand as listing the *only* bases for a conclusion—here, that the list of three items exhausted all the "essential elements" of a jury.

Hughes then turned to the rest of the Sixth Amendment, which set "requirements as to speed, publicity," confrontation with witnesses, and more. And then Hughes pretty expressly disclaimed originalism: "it would hardly be contended that, in all these matters, regard must be had to the particular forms and procedure used at common law"—that is, at the time of the Sixth Amendment's adoption. What mattered was "substance, not . . . form," and the Court's task was to apply the amendment to "achieve[]" its "true purpose." He quoted a recent case involving the Seventh Amendment's guaranty of jury trials in civil cases: "New devices may be used to adapt the ancient institution to present needs and to make of it an efficient instrument in the administration of justice." That "principle of construction" had been applied in criminal cases as well. When Congress enacted statutes dealing with the composition of juries in criminal cases, it could "readjust[] procedures consistent with [the Sixth Amendment's] spirit and purpose" as long as it "safeguard[ed] the essence of the constitutional requirements."

The rest of Hughes's opinion was devoted to explaining why

allowing government employees to serve on criminal juries unless they were actually biased satisfied that requirement. At its heart was a long paragraph opening with the question, "Why should it be assumed that a juror, merely because of employment by the government, would be biased against the accused?" In ordinary criminal trials like Wood's, "It is difficult to see why a governmental employee, merely by virtue of his employment, is interested in that enforcement either more or less than any good citizen is or should be.... What possible interest [in ordinary criminal cases] has a governmental employee different from that of any citizen who wishes to see crime properly punished ... ?"

In the course of this discussion Hughes referred to "the factual situation" in Washington, where there were many potential jurors employed by the government "whose service, by reason of their intelligence and character, would be highly desirable." Hughes thought this point important enough to repeat in his final paragraph on the Sixth Amendment, describing the situation as a "spectacle."

Though *Wood* is shot through with references to material from around the time of the Constitution, we shouldn't see it as an originalist opinion in constitutional theory terms. Nobody denies that references to that sort of thing occurred throughout our constitutional history. Originalism as a constitutional theory requires more than mere references. It requires that those materials drive the opinion.

The "reasoned judgment" alternative to originalism isn't a theory with a single set of simple axioms. "Reasoned judgment" uses many different forms of legal analysis to support the result. *Use* here means that stuff isn't simply sprinkled in for decorative purposes. The question in *Wood* is whether Hughes actually used non-originalist stuff.

The answer is pretty clearly yes. Hughes's discussion of Blackstone wasn't truly originalist. An originalist would say, as Hughes did, that the framers were familiar with Blackstone and adopted his interpretation of many legal issues. Why not this one? Because, as Hughes described it, Blackstone was *wrong*. Blackstone wrote that challenges to jurors in criminal cases were available on the same grounds as in civil cases, where a party's employees were disqualified. And no one denied that an ordinary reader of the passage would say that it meant that the king's employees were disqualified. But, Hughes said, Blackstone didn't refer specifically to this issue in criminal cases—"makes no mention" of actual practice.

Perhaps an originalist could torture Hughes's statement that Blackstone's "omission to mention the case of crown servants cannot be regarded as a sufficient basis" for the interpretation Wood wanted. If you try you can make it into an argument that Blackstone's position was so idiosyncratic that it didn't contribute anything to the original public understanding. I've given you what I hope is a fair summary of Hughes's opinion, and I don't think that's the most natural reading of Hughes's treatment of Blackstone.

And even if I'm wrong about that, Hughes's goal of implementing the Sixth Amendment's "purpose" was clearly policy-based, as shown by his final reference to the "spectacle" of excluding all federal employees from juries. Anyone familiar with the problem would know that here Hughes was alluding to the fact that there were *lots* of these potential jurors. Excluding them would indeed turn criminal trials in the District of Columbia into a spectacle of decision by lower-quality juries. And, to emphasize the point that the policy-based argument did some real work, Hughes made it effectively the opinion's final paragraph.[2]

2. Three sentences followed the policy-based argument, all tersely stating conclusions that, Hughes said correctly, obviously flowed from "what has been said."

Notably, in the gun control cases commonly offered as exemplars of originalist decision-making, Justices Scalia, Alito, and Thomas expressly disclaimed the relevance of policy considerations in interpreting the Constitution. Here's Justice Scalia in the *Heller* case: "We are aware of the problem of handgun violence in this country. . . . But the enshrinement of constitutional rights necessarily takes certain policy choices off the table." Justice Alito in the follow-up *Macdonald* case: *Heller* "specifically rejected" a test that "would require judges to assess the costs and benefits of firearms restrictions and thus to make difficult empirical judgments in an area in which they lack expertise." And Justice Thomas in *Bruen*, restating Justice Alito's point: "federal courts tasked with making such difficult empirical judgments regarding firearm regulations . . . often defer to the determinations of legislatures. . . . [I]t is not deference that the Constitution demands here. . . . It is this balance—struck by the traditions of the American people—that demands our unqualified deference." Hughes's policy-based defense of the result in *Wood* is foreign to modern originalism.

As we'll see in Chapter 4, some versions of originalism allow for updating original understandings. Under those versions the constitution's language—in the cases we'll look at, either the equal protection clause or the clauses referring to citizenship—was understood to enact "what equality really is even if we don't fully understand its content right now." As we get a better understanding of the real *meaning* of equality, our interpretation of the Constitution changes, but we are still enforcing the Constitution as originally understood. Hughes's discussion of "adapt[ing] . . . ancient institution[s]" might be treated as an example of this sort of originalism. We could paraphrase Hughes like this: "People understood that when they placed the term 'trial by jury' in the Constitution they were constitutionalizing what a 'jury' really is—which is, an 'efficient instrument in the administration of justice.'"

I'm skeptical about whether this move is truly available in connection with a fairly concrete noun ("jury") rather than an abstract idea ("equal protection of the laws"). The modern Court has used the move, though, in rejecting the argument that the word "arms" in the Second Amendment referred to "weapons actually available in the founding generation." Instead it interpreted the word to mean "weapons generally available for purposes of self-defense."

Yet, making this sort of move converts originalism from a single-component theory to a theory with two components: original understandings as they actually were and original understandings updated as authorized by the original understanding of abstract terms and some concrete nouns. We might wonder whether that's different in any material way from a pluralist theory—which is to say, in any way that actually limits the power of today's judges to read their own values into the Constitution, which we'll see is one of the things that a theory of interpretation is supposed to do.

The point here isn't that *Wood* was a "living Constitution" decision, but rather that it was a pluralist or eclectic one or, better, one that didn't rely on constitutional theory at all. Some originalists claim for their camp decisions like *Wood* because the Court's references to policy support its originalist analysis. For them to show that a decision is truly pluralist you'd have to show that it used policy (or other non-originalist considerations) to override the meaning revealed by originalist analysis. It seems to me more sensible to say that a decision is pluralist when a number of ways of dealing with the material actually do some analytic work—and, in particular, that the non-originalist material isn't just thrown in as decoration or to show the framers' wisdom in using a term that made good policy sense.

If we were able to ask Hughes to describe his opinion, I'm pretty sure he would say that he included lots of detail about the legal situation around the time of the framing because it increased the opinion's persuasive power, but not that those materials in themselves *had to be* the opinion's foundation. Here they happened to be particularly rich and pretty much spoke with a single voice. But, I think Hughes would have continued, if these materials were more equivocal he would have played up the policy-based reasons that *also* mattered to him.

Wood isn't really an originalist opinion in a constitutional theory sense. At most it's "originalist-ish" with a dollop of policy. It's better to see it as an opinion crafted by an extremely talented lawyer to explain in the most persuasive manner available why the Court's result is correct—reasoned judgment at work.

THE FAMOUS CASE OF THE MINNESOTA MORTGAGE MORATORIUM ACT

Daniel Shays had fought in the Revolutionary War. In 1786 he was a farmer in western Massachusetts. Like other farmers he faced serious money problems: He bought farm supplies on credit but, with little hard currency and no paper money circulating in the area, he found it difficult to pay his creditors. Late in the summer he was part of a group that marched on the courts and shut them down, preventing them from hearing cases brought by creditors against delinquent borrowers. In January 1787, concerned that the state's militia members might sympathize with the rebellious farmers, Boston's business community financed an armed force of about 4,400 men to be deployed against the rebels. Armed with guns and pitchforks, Shays's rebels marched on an arsenal in Springfield, where they were repelled by force. Eventually Shays fled to Vermont. (He was pardoned in 1788.)

The men who drafted the Constitution thought that Shays's Rebellion, as it came to be called, was just the kind of thing that a new national government had to worry about—and prevent if possible. They saw resonances with Shays's forcible efforts to thwart the collection of debts in efforts in states, particularly Rhode Island, to enact statutes that would provide financial relief to debtors. They responded with a constitutional clause limiting state power to enact debtor relief laws: no state shall "pass any . . . Law impairing the Obligation of Contracts." This contracts clause was one of a handful of provisions limiting the power of *states* by protecting individual rights—here the property rights of creditors.[3]

Whenever the economy experienced a serious downturn, debtors rushed to state legislatures for relief. And, because debtors generally outnumbered creditors, state legislators often counted the votes and did what they could to help debtors. Sometimes they extended the time debtors had to pay their debts. Sometimes they protected assets from seizure to pay off debt. They came up with other techniques that helped debtors and hurt creditors, at least in the short run.

These laws were, again typically, almost always challenged immediately as violations of the contracts clause. They did seem to be almost pristine violations of the contracts clause: You signed a contract saying that on July 1 you'd pay back the money you borrowed and the state now says that you don't have to pay until the end of December. That sure looks like an "impairment" of your "obligation." And, beyond the clause's words was its history. Debtor-relief laws were pretty much exactly what the Constitution's drafters had in mind when they wrote the contracts clause.

Throughout the nineteenth century, courts regularly batted down these debtor-relief statutes. Yet when depressed economic

3. The Constitution did give *Congress* the power to enact bankruptcy laws, but Congress held back from exercising that power. It did enact a statute in 1800 allowing commercial traders to be forced into bankruptcy but repealed it in 1803. Broader but still limited bankruptcy acts were adopted in 1841 (repealed in 1843) and 1867 (repealed in 1878).

conditions hit the Midwest in the 1920s, political pressure to "do something" once again proved irresistible. After World War I, European food markets began to recover, and demand for U.S. agricultural products dropped, causing real economic stress in the farm sector. Shays's Rebellion was reproduced as farmers in Iowa and Minnesota blockaded roads and, as before, marched on courthouses to force the suspension of debt-collection lawsuits. The economic crisis in farming in the 1920s, exacerbated by the general depression that began in 1929, produced the usual responses. Farmers in Minnesota and elsewhere put pressure on state legislatures by organizing farm "holidays" during which farmers stopped shipping their products (and sometimes enforced the holidays by blocking the roads). They also revived the old tactics of preventing foreclosure sales by intimidating buyers at foreclosure auctions and sometimes by shutting down courthouses by force.

The Farmer-Labor Party won control of Minnesota's legislature in 1933 and promptly did what state legislatures had done in the past. It enacted a mortgage moratorium act, to be effective until 1935. The act allowed farmers and homeowners who couldn't come up with their mortgage payments to get the courts to suspend foreclosures that their lenders wanted. Before 1933 people whose property had been foreclosed had one year to buy the property back. The act of 1933 gave the courts the power to extend that "redemption" period to two years. In making such an order, the court could require the debtors to pay a "reasonable" portion of what they owed.

John and Rosella Blaisdell had a mortgage on the large house they owned in Minneapolis. Before the depression they managed to pay their monthly mortgage by renting rooms in the house to boarders. The depression cut off the flow of income from the boarders, and the Blaisdells defaulted on their payments. Their bank foreclosed on the house. The Blaisdells couldn't come up with the money to redeem their house, but fortunately for them, the new statute took effect about two weeks before they would have lost their home to the bank. They ran to court and got an order extending the redemption period for a year.

The court told the Blaisdells to pay the bank $40 a month—a seemingly trivial reduction from the $41.80 they hadn't been able to pay when the bank foreclosed. Much more was at stake for banks in Minnesota, of course, and the lender in this case promptly went to the Supreme Court. The language of the contracts clause, the reasons for including it in the Constitution, and the cases interpreting it in the nineteenth century seemed to give banks a strong hand.

They lost, though. Hughes's opinion for the Court shows what judging without theory looks like. Here are some things Hughes expressly *didn't* do.

Not originalism. Hughes didn't deny that the Minnesota mortgage moratorium looked a lot like the kinds of things that led to the Constitution's drafters to include the contracts clause in the first place. His opinion had a paragraph specifically referring to "the reasons which led to the [clause's] adoption. . . . The widespread distress following the revolutionary period, and the plight of debtors, had called forth in the States an ignoble array of legislative schemes for the defeat of creditors and the invasion of contractual obligations."

That wasn't enough to "fix the [clause's] precise scope." "If, by the statement that what the Constitution meant at the time of its adoption it means today, it is intended to say that the great clauses of the Constitution must be confined to the interpretation which the framers, with the conditions and outlook of their time, would have placed upon them, the statement carries its own refutation." This looks a lot like an express rejection of originalism. Maybe not, though, because Hughes continued, "Nor is it helpful to attempt to draw a fine distinction between the intended meaning of the words of the Constitution and their intended application." A contemporary originalist could live with this, and what preceded it, if it's taken as a rejection of what we'll see in Chapter 4 is called original-intended-applications originalism.

No emergency exception. Hughes didn't say that the special economic conditions of the depression in themselves—what lawyers of the time were calling "emergency" conditions—gave governments the power to override the contracts clause. "While emergency does not create power, emergency may furnish the occasion for the exercise of power." That's clearly right. Governments have lots of powers they don't use routinely but bring into play when circumstances—emergencies, for example—making doing something imperative. A virus that might make some people who drink milk a little sick to their stomach might not lead to a quarantine of all infected cows; a mutation that made lots of people very sick might: The mutation "furnishes the occasion for the exercise of [a] power" the government already had.

No updating the text. And, most important, Hughes didn't say that modern economic conditions had made the contract clause outdated. Justice Benjamin Cardozo pressed him on this point, drafting a proposed concurring opinion referring to "economic and social changes wrought by the industrial revolution" that "made it necessary for government of this day to do a thousand things that were beyond the experience of the thought of a century ago." Cardozo acknowledged that his analysis "may be inconsistent with things that men said in 1787," because "[t]hey did not see the changes . . . that lay hidden in the womb of time." But, he continued, their "beliefs to be significant must be adjusted to the world they knew. . . . It is not . . . inconsistent with what they would say today, nor with what they would believe, if they were called upon to interpret . . . the constitution that they framed for the needs of an expanding future."

Though you can twist this into a form of originalism, it's most naturally read as an argument for updating constitutional interpretations in light of changes that emerged from the womb of time. Hughes wasn't unsympathetic to Cardozo's approach—and he needed Cardozo's vote to hold a slim five-to-four majority together. But, for Hughes, Cardozo went too far.

After rejecting original-intended-applications originalism, Hughes seems to invoke a distinction between a general idea—what we'll see in Chapter 4 described as a "concept"—and its implementation in a specific "conception": "The vast body of law which has been developed was unknown to the fathers, but it is believed to have preserved the essential content and the spirit of the Constitution." And the reasons for that development were Cardozo's:

> The settlement and consequent contraction of the public domain, the pressure of a constantly increasing density of population, the interrelation of the activities of our people and the complexity of our economic interests, have inevitably led to an increased use of the organization of society in order to protect the very bases of individual opportunity. Where, in earlier days, it was thought that only the concerns of individuals or of classes were involved, and that those of the State itself were touched only remotely, it has later been found that the fundamental interests of the State are directly affected, and that the question is no longer merely that of one party to a contract as against another, but of the use of reasonable means to safeguard the economic structure upon which the good of all depends.

This was copied almost verbatim from Cardozo's draft concurrence. Notably, it's only inches away from saying that policy can indeed override original meaning.

But if this is what Hughes didn't do, what did he do?

Basically he said that if you looked at the Court's prior decisions carefully the Minnesota statute was no big deal. The Court's task was to construe the clause. "The inescapable problems of construction have been: what is a contract? What are the obligations of contracts? What constitutes impairment of these obligations? What residuum of power is there still in the States in relation to the operation of contracts, to protect the vital interests of the community?" The precedents provided the answers to those questions—and to the one before the Court.

Essentially all of the precedents struck down debtor-relief statutes. Hughes analyzed the cases and showed that each one gave a specific reason for finding the statute unconstitutional: This one permanently changed the debtor's obligation to the lender, that one allowed the debtor to pay nothing at all to the lender, a third simply changed the manner in which the lender got a remedy for the debtor's default. Hughes took the precedents to establish an exclusive list of the ways in which a debtor-relief statute could violate the contracts clause. And, checking off the boxes on the list, Hughes concluded that the Minnesota statute didn't have any of the defects the Court had identified in the precedents.

Hughes ended the core of his opinion with five numbered paragraphs explaining how the Minnesota statute was consistent with the contracts clause as it had been interpreted.

1. A key principle in the precedents was that states always had a "reserved power . . . to protect the vital interests of the community." The economic emergency triggered that reserved power.

2. Another principle was that statutes "for the mere advantage of particular individuals" were bad but not statutes "for the protection of a basic interest of society." For Hughes the Minnesota statute did just that.

3. According to the precedents, debtor-relief statutes had to "be of a character appropriate to th[e] emergency, and could be granted only upon reasonable conditions." The Minnesota statute built conditions into its structure.

4. The conditions were reasonable ones. Debtors still had to pay off their debts and interest continued to accrue. The Blaisdells still had to pay the $40 the lower court said was the reasonable rental value of the house.

5. "The legislation is temporary in operation," expiring in 1935.

There's a lot that can be said about Hughes's opinion, and Justice George Sutherland's dissent said most of it. Hughes never really explains why the Minnesota statute isn't for the benefit of "particular individuals" in just the same way that earlier debtor-relief statutes were. He doesn't explain why the Minnesota statute isn't unconstitutional because it's just shy of resting on bad reason numbers 1, 2, and 3 (two-thirds of three separate bad reasons might add up to two bad reasons in total). And he certainly doesn't explain why the list of bad reasons is exhaustive.

And yet—Hughes's opinion is a terrific piece of judicial craft. It deals quite skillfully with all the relevant legal materials—text (the clause has to be construed), history (the clause's background purposes and aims), precedents. It's not perfect, as I've noted, but I don't think we have any reason to believe that a theory-driven opinion would have been better, and it might well have been a lot worse, for example by woodenly dealing with original expected applications.

And, finally, there's the bottom line: Of course we can say that allowing broad debtor-relief statutes might make it harder for people to borrow money in the future as lenders raise interest rates to adjust for the possibility that they'll be blind-sided by a debtor-relief statute. And indeed there's some evidence that this happened in the 1930s, although the evidence isn't specifically tied to the Minnesota statute. The same study concluded that debtor-relief statutes did let a fair number of farmers hold on to their farms. A study of the Minnesota statute's effects concluded that a "surprisingly small number" of debtors took advantage of the statute—maybe because people like the Blaisdells who couldn't manage to pay $41.80 a month couldn't pay $40 a month either.

In the face of this empirical uncertainty it would be fanatical to say that Hughes's opinion reached a socially undesirable result— and even more fanatical to say that constitutional theory would have led to a better one.

THE "SWITCH IN TIME" CASE
OF JONES & LAUGHLIN

The Minnesota Mortgage Moratorium case suggested that the Court might be comfortable with a range of legislation respond- ing to different ways in which the Great Depression hurt ordinary families. Eventually the Court sided with the New Deal, but the path to that end wasn't smooth.

Franklin Roosevelt's administration tried many things to get the country back on a solid economic footing. Nearly all of them faced heavy opposition from conservatives. The most effective were straightforward spending programs to boost the economy. For technical reasons (the law of "standing," if you want to know), it was basically impossible to bring constitutional challenges to these programs. Conservative businessmen organized the Amer- ican Liberty League to support challenges to as much of the New Deal as they could.

It took several years for these challenges to reach the Court. In 1935 and 1936, though, the Court held a number of FDR's ini- tiatives unconstitutional. The doctrinal bases varied. Here I'll focus on one. The administration said that the programs were constitutional exercises of Congress's power to regulate "Commerce among the several States"—the "interstate commerce" clause. The National Industrial Recovery Act (NIRA) of 1933 regulated wages for wholesalers who sold chickens to grocery stores for cooking at home. Hughes for the Court held that this wasn't a permissible regulation of interstate commerce because, as Hughes put it, the chickens "had come to a permanent rest within the state." The Bituminous Coal Act regulated wages and hours in mining. Here too the Court said no. Justice George Sutherland wrote, "Mining brings the subject matter of commerce into existence. Commerce disposes of it." Hughes agreed with that holding.[4]

The Roosevelt administration had already given up on the NIRA as a depression-fighting tool but it still was committed to regulating wages and hours and, even more important politically, to supporting labor unions by requiring that employers bargain with them. The National Labor Relations Act of 1935 required employers to engage in collective bargaining with workers who chose to organize themselves into unions. The American Liberty League's lawyers insisted that the NLRA was just as unconstitutional as the NIRA and the Coal Act were.

Roosevelt decided to take on what he called the "horse and buggy" Court during his reelection campaign in 1936. He didn't talk much about the Supreme Court itself. Instead he used the American Liberty League as his stalking horse, though it was clear that his attacks on it were challenges to the Court as well. His massive victory in November 1936 led him to put on the table an idea that had been circulating in Washington for several years—

---

4. Hughes wrote a separate opinion disagreeing with other parts of Sutherland's opinion and didn't expressly say that he agreed with the sentences I've quoted. What he did write was this: "production—in this case, mining—which precedes commerce is not itself commerce." In substance, this is Sutherland's point.

expand ("pack") the Court to ensure that it had enough justices favorable to the New Deal's constitutional basis to guarantee that statutes like the NLRA would be upheld.

The saga of the Court-packing plan has been told repeatedly. It failed, but it was a closer call than the usual account has it. One element in the story is what's come to be known as the "switch in time" ("that saved the nine"). Having voted to strike down the NIRA and the Coal Act in 1935 and 1936, Hughes and Justice Owen Roberts voted to uphold the NLRA. Scholars disagree about whether they were somehow influenced or intimidated by the Court-packing plan. For what it's worth, my view is that the plan had some effect on Hughes's thinking (and that Hughes brought Roberts along), but that so many factors were at work that even characterizing what happened as a "switch" is probably misleading.

To see whether constitutional theory helps us understand Hughes's opinion in the NLRA case we must once again get into the doctrinal weeds. In 1937 the doctrine about Congress's power to regulate interstate commerce had three branches. Congress could regulate the "instrumentalities" of interstate commerce, such as railroads. That branch doesn't matter here. Or Congress could regulate the "flow" or "stream" of commerce. Or, finally, Congress could regulate local commerce if that commerce had a "direct" effect on interstate commerce.

Hughes made a case involving the Jones & Laughlin Steel Company the vehicle for the lead opinion upholding the NLRA. Jones & Laughlin was the nation's fourth-largest steel manufacturer. Hughes opened his opinion with a description of Jones & Laughlin's operations at its plant in Aliquippa, Pennsylvania, where the case arose. The description, drawn from the findings made by the National Labor Relations Board, runs across two full pages, and needn't be quoted fully here. Some phrases give a flavor of the discussion: Jones & Laughlin "is a completely integrated enterprise, owning and operating ore, coal, and limestone properties"; it "operates towboats and steam barges used in carrying coal to its factories"; "Much of its product is shipped to its warehouses in Chicago, Detroit, Cincinnati, and Memphis"; "Approximately 75 percent. of its product is shipped out of Pennsylvania."

The effect of this description on ordinary readers should be clear: If *this* isn't something engaged in interstate commerce, what is? The metaphors of a "flow" or "stream" of commerce almost leap from the page. Hughes discussed that branch of commerce clause doctrine but, strikingly, he didn't rely on it: "We find it unnecessary to determine" whether that branch was enough to support the NLRA.

The reason is that the NIRA and Coal Act cases created a serious doctrinal embarrassment. Those cases took advantage of one feature of the metaphors: Flows and streams begin somewhere and end somewhere else. According to the Coal Act case, mining, or, in Hughes's word, production, ended before the stream of commerce began; according to the NIRA case, the stream ended once the goods finally came to rest within a state at the wholesalers. Jones & Laughlin *produced* steel at its plants. The stream of commerce hadn't begun when its workers converted iron ore into steel.

Hughes had another card up his sleeve, the third branch of commerce clause doctrine. Congress could regulate activities that had "direct" effects on interstate commerce. FDR's lawyers had tried to play that card in the Coal Act case: Low wages or long hours at mines or factories, they said, directly affected interstate commerce because low-paid or exhausted miners wouldn't dig as much coal as better-paid and vigorous ones. And that reduction in coal production could be quite large because there were a lot of miners who wouldn't work as hard.

Justice Sutherland said no. For him directness was a conceptual category, not a quantitative one. You had to ask whether setting the wages for a single worker directly affected interstate commerce. True, government could make a plausible case that low wages and long hours might lead to reduced work effort, and reduced work effort might lead to less coal being sent across state lines. But, Sutherland said, that was an *indirect* effect of low wages and long hours—as perhaps shown by the fact that you have to spell out the chain of effects before you get to state lines.

The American Liberty League certainly thought this was enough to dispose of the NLRA as well. It was wrong because Hughes found that wages and hours were different from collective bargaining. Drawing on an argument that the Justice Department lawyer Robert Stern had developed, Hughes said that the point of collective bargaining was to avoid strikes whose very purpose was to disrupt interstate commerce and place pressure on employers to agree: No collective bargaining gives you strikes that *immediately* affected interstate commerce, without any fancy arguments about causal chains. Hughes joined the word "immediate," appropriate for the conceptual account of "direct effects," with the word "catastrophic," appropriate for the quantitative account.

Just before he launched into his discussion of "direct effects," Hughes dismissed the Coal Act case: It held the Coal Act "invalid upon several grounds" and for that reason was "not controlling here." In that phrase he converted a decision supported by *alternative* holdings into one that relied on something he didn't clearly describe but perhaps was something like a group of considerations that cumulatively made the statute unconstitutional.

Now to constitutional theory. Hughes made heavy use of Framing-era materials in *Wood* to make his opinion rhetorically persuasive without committing himself to originalism as constitutional theory. His opinion in *Jones & Laughlin* shows him again at his rhetorical finest *and* without much originalism. His opening description of Jones & Laughlin's operations might have suggested that an enterprise so large had to be engaged in interstate commerce in a way captured by the "flow of commerce" metaphor: Iron ore flowed into Aliquippa, was made into steel, and flowed out on the railroads and barges to Detroit and Memphis. Having created this image in his readers' minds, Hughes switched horses as the opinion proceeded and adopted a quite different doctrine. He did treat "direct effects" as a conceptual category, but here too the framing emphasizing Jones & Laughlin's size surely brought the quantitative idea back into play. As in *Wood*, Hughes constructed an opinion around persuasive arguments, not theory.

That Hughes was engaged in an exercise in persuasion, not theory, is driven home by the following facts. *Jones & Laughlin* was only one of five cases the Court decided on April 12, 1937, rejecting challenges to the NLRA. Another was *NLRB v. Friedman-Harry Marks Clothing Co.* It involved a small company that made men's clothing in Virginia and shipped the garments to New York and elsewhere for retail sale—it had about 800 employees, in contrast with Jones & Laughlin's 10,000 in its Pennsylvania plant, and sales of $1.75 million in 1935, contrasted with Jones & Laughlin's position as a major player in the steel industry. Like his opinion in *Jones & Laughlin*, Hughes's opinion for the Court in *Friedman-Harry Marks* set out the NLRB's findings, suggesting that the rhetorical power of the opening of the *Jones & Laughlin* opinion was sort of inadvertent—Hughes was using a template not tailored to the particular case. He then offered this legal analysis: "For reasons stated in our opinion in *Jones & Laughlin* . . . , we hold that the objections raised by [Friedman-Harry Marks] . . . are without merit." Period. His four dissenting colleagues' rhetorical counter was to make *Friedman-Harry Marks*, not *Jones & Laughlin*, the vehicle for their dissent.

THE PROTO-"THEORY" CASE
OF *CAROLENE PRODUCTS*

Almost before there was originalism there was John Hart Ely. In 1980, Ely, a professor at Harvard Law School, published *Democracy and Distrust,* a classic in constitutional theory, hugely influential among academics in the United States and judges and academics around the world. Against what he called "clause-bound interpretivism"—the name he gave to what was then originalism in a nascent form—Ely offered "representation-reinforcing review." That kind of review would view with great skepticism laws that were likely to prevent the "outs" from replacing the "ins" through ordinary electoral politics—restrictions on voting rights for disfavored groups, limitations on free expression rights to criticize the policies the government was pursuing, and quite a bit more. But, importantly, it wouldn't get liberals of the 1980s and after everything: Without doing some fancy footwork it wouldn't get you the right to choose with respect to abortion, or marriage equality.

Ely had clerked for Earl Warren and he thought that the Warren Court's best work embodied representation-reinforcing review. Such review didn't start with the Warren Court, though. As Ely of course acknowledged, its origins were in a footnote in a case decided in 1938.

To be literate in constitutional theory you have to be able to rattle off "*Carolene Products* footnote 4." Carolene Products produced "filled milk," a form of evaporated milk with added vitamins that was cheaper than whole milk and could be used in a wider variety of ways than ordinary milk. Responding to the farm crisis of the 1920s, which hit milk production with real force, and concerned about losing market share, milk producers got Congress to pass a law prohibiting the sale of filled milk, arguing speciously that the vitamins in filled milk didn't do as much to promote good health as the same vitamins in whole milk.

In an opinion by Justice Harlan Fiske Stone, the Supreme Court held the statute constitutional. That was no big deal by 1938, when as a result of the switch in time the Court had basically abandoned the attempt to subject economic regulations to any but the most cursory judicial scrutiny. Indeed, the newly appointed Justice Hugo Black concurred only in the result because he detected a hint in Stone's opinion that it left open the possibility that some-day somewhere some lower court could hold a trial to determine whether there was in fact some basis in the real world for thinking that an economic regulation actually didn't accomplish anything. (As it happened, a generation later, in 1972, a lower court relied on developments in the technology of milk production to find that filled milk was just as health-promoting as whole milk and that the statute was—had become?—unconstitutional.)

Stone had been playing with an idea probably raised initially by his former law school colleague and long-term correspondent Thomas Reed Powell, who had by then moved to Harvard Law School, and reinforced by conversations with his law clerk Louis Lusky. The core idea was later developed in detail by Ely: Courts should step in only when there was some reason to think both that ordinary political processes had misfired *and* that you couldn't rely on those same processes to undo the mistake. Stone floated the idea in an opinion for the Court published several weeks before *Carolene Products*. Lusky then drafted a more elaborate version for use there.

The first sentence of Lusky's draft footnote referred to "the corrective political processes which can ordinarily be expected to bring about the repeal of unwise legislation." The next sentence gave as examples laws "interfer[ing] with political organization and with the dissemination of information." After two additional sentences, Lusky's draft said, "It may be too that when a statute is directed at a religious, a national, or a racial minority, the usual corrective processes will be hampered."

Stone reworked Lusky's draft into two paragraphs. The first was a clearer version of Lusky's initial sentence and threw in references to nine cases. The second picked up the theme of discrimination and added to Lusky's mention of race and religion the possibility of "prejudice against discrete and insular minorities." Then Stone sent the draft to his colleagues.

And here's where *our* story gets interesting. Chief Justice Hughes was "somewhat disturbed" by the footnote. He thought that its discussion of free expression cases overlooked the fact that in those cases the statutes were "directly opposed to the constitutional guaranty"—and, his phrasing implied, could be held unconstitutional without invoking the concerns about the political process that the draft footnote focused on. Stone immediately responded by adding a new first paragraph: "There may be narrower scope for operation of the presumption of constitutionality when legislation appears on its face to be within a specific prohibition of the Constitution, such as those of the first ten Amendments."

Taken together the footnote's three paragraphs were expressly methodologically pluralist. Seen in constitutional theory terms the first paragraph was textualist, the second and third representation-reinforcing. Note that the first paragraph appears to sweep in *all* textual guarantees, so that the second and third have to refer to some non-textual constitutional rights. (Note as well that textualism isn't originalism, though it's a close relative.)

Carolene Products footnote 4 teaches these lessons:

- The footnote is only a *proto-constitutional theory*. Years later Lusky pointed out, accurately, that it was after all only a footnote and was written in highly conditional terms. Stone was trying out an idea that Ely worked up into a constitutional theory.

- The footnote recognizes the possibility, perhaps even the inevitability, of constitutional *rights not tied to the text.*
- And, most important, it shows that even when constitutional theory cropped up in embryonic form in the 1930s, it was *pluralist* in ways thought dangerous by today's originalist theory.

LEARNING FROM THE PAST

The most important lesson I take from these cases is that they weren't theory-driven at all. Perhaps they can be described as pluralist, though even there the components are mostly proto-theories, as in *Carolene Products.* To pick up on our imagined conversation with Hughes, he would have been baffled, I believe, by the question, "What constitutional theories do you use?" Perhaps after resolving his puzzlement he would say something like, "I try to interpret the Constitution to make it a suitable instrument for governance in today's United States." The next chapter argues that this turns out to be a pretty decent explanation of what an uncapitalized constitutional theory should be about, but it doesn't focus specifically on constitutional interpretation.

If we continued to press Hughes, perhaps he would respond, "I try to write *good* opinions." Here "good" refers to the virtues associated with skillful lawyering. When the opinions are good, they are rhetorically powerful. The arguments grapple fairly with the precedents both for and against the opinion's result. Sometimes that's done well, sometimes not so well; compare here *Wood's* treatment of the 1909 case (good) with the Blaisdell case's treatment of the list of precedents (not so good) and *Jones & Laughlin's* treatment of "manufacturing precedes commerce" (also not so good). Most important, they use as many of the materials of legal argument—text, precedent, constitutional structure, policy, traditions—as those who join the opinion find helpful. And they use those materials in varying mixes depending on the issues raised by the case and how helpful the materials of each type are in crafting a persuasive opinion.

The word "craft" is key. Some aspects of craft are straightforward.

A well-crafted opinion is as *transparent* as possible: It displays on its surface (or with only a little digging by the reader) the considerations that the opinion's author believes to be analytically important. One important consequence of transparency is that a careful reader can see just where the opinion bumps up against a really difficult, perhaps intractable problem. (Recall Hughes's line in *Jones & Laughlin* that the Coal Act decision wasn't controlling.)

A well-crafted opinion is dominated by *legal* considerations. What counts as such considerations varies over time, as I'll argue in the Conclusion. But, although a well-crafted opinion can have some rhetorical flourishes, it can't flaunt its rhetoric or style.

A well-crafted opinion deploys a standard set of *legal "moves."* It acknowledges the existence of precedents pointing away from its conclusion but distinguishes those precedents by noting that they contain factual or legal features that help us understand why the precedents don't actually control the case at hand. It also draws strength from cases that are similar but not precisely the same by discerning in them some general principle that extends to the case at hand. The three Hughes opinions described in this chapter show a really talented lawyer in action as he faces up to adverse precedents and bats them away, and sees how to embrace and extend favorable precedents.

A well-crafted opinion keeps its *audience* in mind. For technical cases (of a sort we haven't really examined here), the audience consists of technical specialists, and a well-crafted opinion might be quite opaque to non-specialist readers. For high profile constitutional cases the audience includes what political scientists call "attentive publics." In the 1930s these were legal academics and bar leaders, with a handful of newspaper reporters and editorialists sprinkled in. Today the attentive public includes many more people—bloggers and broadcast journalists, for example—who take the opinions and transmit them to the rest of the citizenry.

Perhaps more controversially: A well-crafted opinion is *respectful* of contrary opinions. A majority opinion doesn't cast aspersions on dissenters. A well-crafted majority opinion doesn't have "zingers." A dissent points out what its author believes to be analytic flaws in the majority opinion but it doesn't sneer at those on the other side as legal ignoramuses.

Writing to his sister a couple of weeks after he had joined the dissent in the Minnesota Mortgage Moratorium case, Justice Willis Van Devanter expressed pride in the role he'd played in shaping Justice Sutherland's dissenting opinion. He ended by noting that he was "extremely disappointed in the outcome of the case . . . but I must refrain from being too intense about this or anything else." Van Devanter was referring specifically to how intensity affected his health. His attitude, though, is entirely commendable. He understood that the justices with whom he disagreed quite vigorously were his colleagues and compatriots, not his enemies. They were wrong but well-meaning. Whatever this attitude's effect was on Van Devanter's physical health, it's a way of thinking that contributes to a healthy polity.

This isn't a comprehensive catalogue of what makes an opinion well-crafted, but it should be enough to suggest that constitutional theory has little to do with whether an opinion is well-crafted. Now for the next step: Instead of saying that an opinion is well-crafted we could say that it displays "reasoned judgment" or "good judgment." We might be tempted to say that "reasoned judgment" *is* a constitutional theory, but we should resist that temptation because doing so would direct our attention away from the criteria of wide experience and intellectual curiosity that really matter.

We'll see, though, that what counts as good judicial craft might be affected by historical circumstances—and, in particular, might change as our constitutional discourse gets polarized.

So far I've been drawing a contrast between judging without theory and judging with it, but I haven't done more than gesture in the direction of what theory actually is by saying that in its current form it's about how judges should interpret the Constitution and, a bit more specifically, includes attention to original meaning as an important, perhaps overriding consideration. The next two chapters provide more systematic accounts of constitutional theory, including theories of interpretation, and of originalism.

CHAPTER 3

What Is Constitutional Theory and Why Should We Care?

Constitutional theory is in the news. Editorial columns and op-ed writers praise or excoriate Supreme Court justices for decisions that the writers and the justices' defenders say are guided by constitutional theory. Originalism and "living constitutionalism" are the leading contenders. Chapter 4 says a fair amount about originalism but otherwise this book stands back from the controversies you find on editorial pages. My argument is that constitutional theory as it's usually presented doesn't help anyone think seriously and systematically about how our judges should decide cases.

First, though, we have to get a handle on the very idea of constitutional theory. That's this chapter's task. First we'll look at constitutional theory in the large, then at its first important subcomponent—its account of the division of labor among our institutions, and particularly between our elected representatives and our judges. Only then will I talk about constitutional theories of interpretation, the typical focus of discourse about constitutional theory. At the end I argue that judging doesn't need even a constitutional theory of interpretation because it's a practice guided not by "rules" of interpretation but by historically contingent yet deeply embedded ideas about the qualities that make a person a good judge.

WHAT CONSTITUTIONAL THEORY IS

Foundational constitutional theory starts with a bunch of people who, for a combination of instrumental reasons and what Lincoln called the "mystic chords of memory," think that they'll be better off cooperating with each other for some indefinite period. They know, though, that they're going to disagree about lots of things—about what the best policies are, of course, but also about what the best institutions are for coming up with those policies. A policy example: Should there be different tax rates for ordinary income and capital gains? An institutional example: Should the capital gains rate be set by the legislature, a specialized agency, or the courts? (And should there be one or two houses in the legislature?) They address these problems with a constitution. And constitutional theory deals with questions about what it means to do that. The question that animates constitutional theory in the United States is this: How can a people be self-governing if they are unable, without extraordinary effort, to obtain from "their" government policies that on reflection and after deliberation a majority of them prefer?

Constitutions divide the overall domain of public policy into two parts. In one, outcomes result from the ordinary cut and thrust of politics. In the other, policy choice is removed from that cut and thrust, to be governed in the first instance by choices made in the past (choices which, in all the interesting cases, a current majority would make differently), though revisable by some special supermajority requirement for amendment.

Because the constitution was written a while ago—more than two centuries, for the United States—the people who wrote it are long gone, replaced by us today. If we were writing a constitution today we might make different choices about how to design some of our institutions—maybe more than two senators for each state, maybe no Senate at all—and about some of the policies our predecessors made, such as a more limited right against self-incrimination in criminal cases.

In principle we can make those choices today by amending the constitution. To do that, though, we have to go through more hoops than we do in the ordinary cut and thrust of politics. And note one often overlooked feature of the very fact that constitutions do allow for their own amendment. Amendment procedures exist because the constitution's authors understood that they might have made mistakes (or that some of their choices might become outdated). The overlooked feature is that they might have been mistaken about the procedures for amending the constitution—perhaps they're well-designed to deal with some proposals for amendment but badly designed for other proposals.

The Constitution as Binding Law

Suppose we understand the constitution as follows: The people who wrote it knew they were working under some time constraints. They devised a constitution that in their judgment would create a government that as it went into operation would produce as good a set of policies as anything else they could think of. Here "good" means something like "consistent with the preferences of the polity at the time within the constraints of fundamental rights." They knew, though, that their understanding of how the constitution would in fact operate once it was up and running might be mistaken, whether because of flaws in the initial design or because of social, technological, and similar changes they knew would occur but the contours of which they couldn't anticipate. They included an amendment rule in the constitution, but they knew that it too might be flawed. As it turned out they did a pretty good job of designing a government and an amendment rule and we've adhered to it over generations for that reason and not because the constitution has some authority over us.

That understanding implies, I think, that the written constitution is a set of recommendations about good governance and that departures from it should be undertaken with some degree of caution. Suppose, though, that social, technological, or other changes give rise to a widespread view that the constitution is flawed in some specific respect. So, for example, people come to think that the constitution sets the minimum age for service in Congress too high: Younger people should be allowed to compete for seats in the House and Senate. Suppose further that the amendment rule requires substantial support from Congress before an amendment takes effect (two-thirds in each house, under the U.S. rule). Maybe members of Congress refuse to provide the support required out of self-interest (they don't want to face additional competition for their seats) or prejudiced views about the deliberative capacity of younger people. Put in slightly more general terms, the amendment rule is flawed but only with respect to the proposal now on the table. And even more generally, the amendment rule might be flawed in different ways with respect to different proposals to alter the constitution-in-place.

An authoritative constitution stymies the proposal's adoption. In principle the proposal's supporters could seek to amend the amendment rule either in general or with respect to this proposal—or even seek to replace the existing constitution with a new one. The proposal's supporters, though, believe that the constitution is quite good overall, just mistaken about the minimum age provision. They don't want to change the amendment rule in general. Amending the amending rule only with respect to their proposal would again be stymied by the amendment rule itself.

The reason I've put the "constitution as recommendation" idea on the table is that it highlights the problem that actually animates constitutional theory in the United States. We don't treat the U.S. Constitution as a set of recommendations about good governance. We treat it as binding law. "Treat" here is the relevant word.[1] We could change our minds.

Indeed, one component of the regime shifts I described in Chapter 1 is often a reconsideration of some of the constitutional principles that seemed deeply embedded: During the Progressive Era, for example, serious questions were raised about judicial supremacy, and at the state level some new institutions were put in place to weaken its hold. Over the past generation presidential impeachment may have moved from being an extraordinary remedy for grave abuses of power to being just another form of congressional oversight of the presidency.

Right now, though, we seem to think that we ought to treat the Constitution as binding law. Even recent pushes for "Court reform" tinker with institutional design—term limits, most notably—without questioning that.

Constitutional Theory and Binding Law

Treating the Constitution as a set of recommendations means this: For any question about policy or institutional design, we go

1. The U.S. Constitution *says* that it is binding law in the Supremacy Clause, Article VI, but saying it can't make it so. Suppose I find ten people in every state who agree with me about writing a new constitution that says *it* is binding law. No one's going to think that it really is—unless other people start treating the Tushnet et al. constitution as law overriding the U.S. Constitution. Shakespeare had it right: When Glendower boasts that he can "call spirits from the vasty deep," Hotspur punctures his pretensions: "Why, so can I, or so can any man; But will they come when you do call for them?" There is a basically unpersuasive argument rattling around that officials who take an oath to support "this Constitution" are required to treat the Constitution as binding law, and even more are required to follow the original understanding of the Constitution's terms. The argument is unpersuasive because it trades on badly elaborated arguments about what the word "this" refers to.

through the following reasoning process. The people who wrote the Constitution were pretty smart about policy and institutional design, and the choices they made have on the whole worked out pretty well. Right now, though, it seems to a majority of us that one of their choices isn't working well. We've talked about their choice, and we've noted our respect for their wisdom. We've also thought pretty hard about the merits of the change we're proposing, and we've let some time pass to make sure that we're not being influenced by the passions of the moment. We've also thought about using the Constitution's own provisions for amendment to get where we want to go. But, again after serious discussion, deliberation, and a waiting period, we've concluded that the amendment procedure is too cumbersome. Taking everything into account, we think that making the change would make our system of government better—would make us better off overall. That's what I'll call the "first order" rule we'd like to follow—or, more informally, the "Do the Right Thing" rule.

We are about to go pretty deep into a forest with a lot of underbrush, and unfortunately the underbrush is important to sustaining the forest's ecology, so we can't simply clear it away. The question we're going to be asking is, "Can 'Do the Right Thing' be the rule we actually use?" At the start of the journey the answer will seem to be, "No." Remember that we come up with a constitution because we disagree with each other about what the Right Thing is. So, it might seem that we need to find something we can agree on that we can then use to come up with provisional, temporary decisions about what to do (the Right Thing from some of our points of view, the Wrong Thing from others).

Constitutions set up institutions—legislatures, executives, courts—that when we disagree we hope will give each of us a fair shot at bringing others to our side on one or another issue. That fair shot sets up a "live and let live" situation: The institutions generate a set of policies that (again, we hope) will Do the Right Thing from our point of view often enough to offset the times when the policies are misguided. Each of us wins some and loses some, but when each of us looks at the overall set of policy outcomes we end up thinking that working with those institutions will do better at coming close to a balance that we can live with than any other institutions we can design. Constitutional theorists call this a principle of institutional settlement.

The primary competitor to some principle of institutional settlement is violence—captured in a line from the movie *Fried Green Tomatoes:* "I'm older and have more insurance." That's an explanation of why one person or group has more power than another, not a reason for exercising that power. And violence can't be ruled out as a response to truly oppressive constitutional arrangements. But, of course, we certainly hope that some principle of institutional settlement will be good enough (for government work) that we're willing to put up with our political losses because we win often enough that netting out the wins and losses and taking the costs of violence into account we think that institutional settlement is the way to go.

Treating the Constitution (including the amendment procedure) as binding law is another reason that sometimes decision-makers think they can't Do the Right Thing. Maybe lots of us—sixty-five percent—think that eliminating the Senate would make us better off overall. The Constitution as binding law says we can't get rid of the Senate without doing an enormous amount of organizing and fancy footwork. The Constitution prevents us from following the first-order rule.

Note, though, that there's a bias built into this scheme. Suppose Congress fails to do the right thing and defeats a proposal that would actually make us better off. We might develop a robust notion that Congress is under some sort of constitutional *duty* to do the right thing but so far in the United States we don't have such a notion readily available.[2] A related bias is built into the courts' role. They can strike down a statute when it tries to do the right thing in a way that's barred by the Constitution as binding law. But—again subject to the possibility of constitutional amendment—we're stuck with the result if the legislature does the right thing and the Court mistakenly says the Constitution means they can't do it.

Constitutional theory is about what we can do as a second-best approach—or, as I'll put it, what are the second-order rules that get us as close as we can to making us better off overall? The principle of institutional settlement moves the ball forward but doesn't get us all the way. The constitution says that legislatures can do some things but implicitly not others, the president has some powers but implicitly not others, and the courts can do some things but not others. We're going to disagree about what those various powers and limitations are. The second-order rules define the contours of the powers and limitations.

The idea behind the second-order rules is the same as the one behind the constitution itself. How can we deal with persistent disagreement, this time not about what the Right Thing is but about the contours of the powers and limitations? As before, by narrowing the range of disagreement.

Here's where theories of interpretation come in. The hope is that we can agree on an approach to interpreting the constitution that narrows the range of disagreement even more, to the point where we can live with the remaining disagreement. Take origi-

2. Other nations do. Portugal's constitution has a provision about "unconstitutionality by omission," though it isn't enforced much. Colombia has a doctrine that allows courts to intervene when there's an "unconstitutional state of affairs," which ordinarily arises when the legislature hasn't done enough to deal with the situation.

nalism as an example. Originalists look for evidence of the original public meaning of the Constitution's terms. There's going to be disagreement about the strength of the inferences to be drawn from that evidence. Was the president's duty to faithfully execute the laws understood to mean that the president had to have the unfettered power to fire any executive official who acted on an understanding of what the laws required that differed from the president's? Roughly speaking this is what the theory of the unitary executive holds. There's a lot of disagreement about whether the historical evidence supports that theory. But disagreement about the strength of that evidence is different from—and in an important sense narrower than—disagreement about what the Right Thing is.

A PRELIMINARY: TWO WAYS OF THINKING ABOUT INTERPRETATION

Most of the time we read something and understand it right away—we don't think of ourselves as "interpreting" the text. The Constitution's "mathematical" provisions are like that. No one worries about what the provision saying "No Person shall be a Senator who shall not have attained to the Age of thirty Years" means, even though real cases have arisen around the fringes of the provision (thirty years old on election day? On the day the elected Senator is sworn in? Some day during the Senator's six-year term?)[3] Only slightly more complicated is a provision that originalists like to cite, the constitutional requirement that Congress protect each state "against domestic Violence." A tiny bit of historical inquiry shows that the provision refers to *public* disorder,

---

3. For what it's worth, the congressional practice appears to be, "On the swearing-in day, with a tiny bit of leeway." The leeway might be based on understandings about travel times and inaccuracies of birth records in the nation's first decades.

not violence within the household—and you probably don't even need the historical inquiry to figure that out, because it's really hard to understand how Congress is supposed to protect *states* against violence within the household.

Interpretation comes into the picture only when we're puzzled about what we're reading. Maybe something strikes us as odd, or unclear, or vague, and under the circumstances we feel some need to figure out what the words really mean—mostly, because we think we have to do something and what we do, we think, should be affected by the words' meaning.

A first way of figuring out what unclear or vague terms mean trades on what some call "homey" examples. Two common ones involve grocery lists and recipes. Suppose someone you know is sick and can't get to the grocery store. The list is something like this: "Organic butter, free range eggs, kale, avocado, cereal." You get to the store and find the first four items in an aisle for organic foods, which also has a number of organic cereals. But, of course, there's another aisle that has lots of heavily sweetened cereals. Do you think you might as well buy a bunch of serving-sized Froot Loops with marshmallows? (I note that today the story would have to be fleshed out even more by explaining why your friend can't get the cereal she really wants by ordering it on-line and having it delivered—an example of how modern technology might affect what counts as an unclear or vague term.)

Here's a recipe example: Your family has a favorite soup recipe. It includes beef stock, lots of carrots and celery, slices of Andouille sausage, and a special ingredient—turmeric. You're planning to make the soup for a family celebration. Before you go to the store to buy the ingredients you happen to read a news story about turmeric. The story suggests that there are some newly discovered health concerns about the spice—and that food scientists have modified some other spice (cardamom, maybe) to give foods a flavor quite similar (according to some tasters even better than) turmeric, with an enhanced "smoky" flavor as well. (You can tell that I know nothing about cooking.) When you make the soup you use the modified cardamom spice. Can you tell your family that you've followed the family tradition in making the soup?

Defenders of "ordinary" interpretation tend to say that you haven't followed the recipe because modified cardamom just isn't turmeric. You've modified (amended) the recipe to make it better for the family but that's different from following it. Maybe your modification (amendment) is somehow authorized but you still shouldn't tell your family that you're serving them the traditional soup. Similarly, defenders of ordinary interpretation tend to say that you wouldn't be doing what your friend wants if you came back with the Froot Loops. And here "wants" is the important word: Ordinary interpretation involves figuring out what the person who wrote the list meant to communicate.

Ordinary interpretation seems fine, even the obvious thing to do, most of the time. We need to think about it a bit more, though. We have to consider what I'll call initially the "social context" within which ordinary interpretation occurs. I'll then abandon that term, mostly because the word "context" as used in discussion of ordinary interpretation tends to mean the larger group of words of which the one we're worrying about occurs. I'll substitute the term "institutional" and say that we always have to think about what words mean by taking their institutional setting into account. For constitutional interpretation the institutions that matter are the elected branches (legislatures and executives) and the courts.

Let's thicken the social context of our shopping-list and recipe examples. You know that your ailing friend and his husband are raising a couple of kids. They think it's important that they model for the kids an "ecologically sensitive" lifestyle. When they take the kids to the grocery store they always confine themselves to the aisles with organic foods. You know, though, that the kids complain a lot about not having the chance to eat the way their friends do, with a fair amount of heavily sweetened foods. If you come back from the shopping trip with the Froot Loops the kids are going to be happy because they'll get a serving-sized Froot Loops breakfast once or twice a week and the parents are going to be secretly relieved (no whining from the kids, no commitment to serving Froot Loops every morning until they run out, no breach of their commitment to model the right lifestyle for them). All in all, you'll have made them better off—you'll have Done the Right Thing.

As to the recipe: You know that your family prides itself on working creatively within the tradition it's established. They'll praise you for following the recipe when you substitute sweet potatoes for carrots or chorizo for Andouille sausage—if the soup tastes good. So too for using the modified cardamom. From the family's point of view following the recipe means working within its basic parameters—some sort of sausage but not diced chicken—to make a good tasting soup. Here too using the modified cardamom is the Right Thing (or at least *a* Right Thing).

These thickened examples show that we can say that interpreting vague or unclear words involves taking into account their social context. The distinction between "following" and "modifying" blurs—or, again, between "interpreting" and "amending."

The institution in the examples is "the family," or more precisely particular families as they have developed over time. So too with the institutions for interpreting the Constitution: The institutions we have to think about are the elected branches and the courts and, importantly, their traditions about what's interpreting and what's amending.

DO ELECTED OFFICIALS NEED CONSTITUTIONAL THEORY? (PROBABLY NOT)

In 1975, Paul Brest, then a young legal scholar (later to be dean of Stanford Law School and chief executive of the Hewlett-Packard

Foundation), published a short article, "The Conscientious Legislator's Guide to Constitutional Interpretation." He pointed out that the Constitution's text seemed to address legislators more than judges. The First Amendment says, for example, that *Congress* shall make no law abridging the freedom of speech. How should a legislator think about the Constitution? Brest ended up offering two guidelines: A legislator shouldn't vote for a legislative proposal solely for the purpose of inflicting harm on some group, and a legislator should vote for a proposal only if she thinks that it advances some public purpose. The first guideline has some modest purchase against racists and other would-be discriminators, the second on laws that do nothing more than express the legislators' distaste for something people are doing—what today is sometimes called a performative exercise. But, overall, the guidelines cover a tiny fraction of cases.

Brest wrote his article before the rise of constitutional theory. Today he'd have to ask whether a conscientious legislator should follow some theory: support proposals only if they are consistent with the original understanding or only if they are consistent with contemporary understandings of fundamental values, for example. The alternative is, once again, the Do the Right Thing rule: A legislator can support proposals if they are in her view the Right Thing for the government to do and oppose them if they aren't.

The Do the Right Thing rule might be better than following even the right constitutional theory (if there is one). Many legislators aren't lawyers and won't do a good job of working out what a constitutional theory has to say about many proposals—and won't be in a good position to evaluate on the merits the arguments proponents and opponents offer to show why the proposal is or isn't consistent with the right constitutional theory.

On this count elected executive officials—presidents and

governors—might be in a better position to think about constitutional theory when they have to sign or veto bills that have gotten through the legislature. They do regularly get legal advice, mostly about how they are supposed to go about faithfully executing the laws. That gives them the opportunity to develop a sense of whether or to what extent they should treat the constitutional advice they're getting as the product of disinterested legal analysis.

Whether the advice is disinterested, though, is always going to be a serious question for both executive officials and legislators. You almost always can come up with plausible arguments that a proposal is or isn't consistent with the constitutional theory you think you should follow (just track either the majority or dissenting opinions in Supreme Court cases on related questions and say that the proposal before either is or isn't distinguishable from the one upheld or struck down by the Court). And, empirically, there seems to be a strong correlation between legislators' views of a bill's policy wisdom and its constitutionality. You almost never find a legislator saying, "This is a really good idea but unfortunately it's unconstitutional." Senator David Boren, a former governor who had and had used a line-item veto when dealing with his state's budget, did say about a proposed federal analogue, "as much as I favor the line-item veto, I feel I have no choice but to vote that it does not comply with the Constitution of the United States." The example is striking because it's so rare.

You do find legislators saying, "This is a really bad idea and fortunately it's unconstitutional." That's pretty common in discussions of gun control bills, for example. It typically comes into play, though, only when the legislator who opposes the bill thinks that there's a real chance that the bill will become law. Then it serves as a warning: "Go ahead and pass it, but in the end the courts are going to strike it down—and we'll campaign against you not simply on the ground that you enacted a bad policy but also on the ground that you knew you were about to violate the Constitution."

Mostly, though, legislators who oppose proposals say simply that they would make us worse rather than better off. They are, that is, the Wrong Thing to Do. If that's okay when you oppose a proposal, maybe the "Do the Right Thing" rule is okay when you support it. Or, put a bit more formally, the conscientious legislator can think that a proposal is constitutional precisely because it's the Right Thing to Do.

There's one additional consideration for elected officials. Their constituents elect them to enact policies that make us better off and to defeat policy proposals that make us worse off. I suppose a legal scholar could write an article, even shorter than Brest's, "The Conscientious Voter's Guide to Constitutional Interpretation." I'm pretty sure that it would offer an even weaker guideline than Brest did for legislators, probably along the lines, "Don't vote for a candidate who you think is likely to support unconstitutional proposals quite a bit of the time." Elected officials may reasonably take the very fact that they've been elected as an indication that their constituents think they will follow the "Do the Right Thing" rule most of the time and thereby make us better off. So, why bother to ask an additional question about whether a proposal runs up against some objection based upon a constitutional theory that's at most a way of trying to implement the "Do the Right Thing" rule?

The Republican majority in the House of Representatives instituted the practice of reading the Constitution at the House's opening session, a practice that expresses their view that they—and presumably not the Democrats in the minority—believe that they have some obligation to take the Constitution into account when they legislate. No one's been able to identify any discernable impact the reading has had on their actual behavior—perhaps because the asserted obligation turns out to be performative and expressive rather than motivational.

Limits on Congressional Constitutional Interpretation?

Recall that the shopping-list and recipe examples involved interpretations rather than amendments because they operated within some basic parameters. That your decisions operate within some basic parameters is important, of course. The Constitution requires that treaties be approved by "two-thirds of the Senators present." Suppose you think that the Senate has seriously messed up U.S. foreign policy by failing to approve important treaties by the constitutionally required two-thirds vote. You can't say, "What the heck, let's adopt a rule of the Senate that says that a treaty approved by Senators representing two-thirds of the nation's population is deemed approved by 'two-thirds of the Senators present and voting.'"

This still leaves room for some creative constitutional workarounds—practices that comply with a constitutional provision but seem somehow like cheating. We've worked around the problem that the two-thirds requirement for treaty approval of course makes it difficult to get a treaty through the Senate. Particularly since 1945, a substitute for treaties has developed: the executive agreement. Executive agreements take two forms. In one the president simply signs the agreement with a foreign nation and thereby commits the United States to complying with its terms. In the other each house of Congress approves the agreement by a majority vote (note that the House gets in on the game, perhaps compensating for the reduction of the required Senate majority from two-thirds to one half).

The executive-agreement workaround leads to another question: Can executive agreements be used to do everything that treaties can? The consensus answer is No. Only treaties, it's thought, can create a binding legal commitment for the United States to come to the aid of a nation attacked by an enemy, and certain kinds of commercial arrangements, it's thought, probably can be made only in a treaty.

The United States doesn't yet have a general account of the limits on constitutional workarounds. Other nations might provide some guidance. Courts in India pioneered in developing a "basic structure" doctrine, holding that some constitutional amendments that were adopted in a procedurally regular manner were nonetheless unconstitutional because they undermined the constitution's basic structure. Workarounds are acceptable because they aren't inconsistent with the point of the provisions they work around. This points in the direction of something like a "basic structure" limit on constitutional workarounds.

WHY JUDGES MIGHT NEED CONSTITUTIONAL THEORY (AND WHY THEY PROBABLY CAN'T GET WHAT THEY NEED FROM IT)

Dissenting from the Court's holding unconstitutional Connecticut's ban on using contraceptives, Justice Potter Stewart called the statute "an uncommonly silly law" but said that he couldn't find any basis for holding it unconstitutional. His policy views about the statute's wisdom were different from his views about its constitutionality. I've argued that elected officials are likely to bring their policy and constitutional views into close alignment. And generations of political scientists have shown that Supreme Court justices' policy and constitutional views are correlated. In one widely quoted formulation, "[William] Rehnquist votes the way he does because he is extremely conservative; [Thurgood] Marshall votes the way he does because he is extremely liberal." Justice Stewart's comment suggests, though, that the correlation for justices is weaker than that for elected politicians. That leaves some space for law to operate.

How can justices work things out so that "the law" overall reflects the best combination of their policy and constitutional views? Here's where constitutional theory comes in.

To simplify the story, I'm going to tell it as if we had only a single Supreme Court justice. Despite that, you should keep in mind the story makes sense only if its subject, Justice X, manages to get four other justices to go along with her often enough to let me say that Justice X's position is "the Court's" position. As the story reaches its conclusion I'll replace "Justice X" with "the five justices who form the Court's majority most of the time" and connect the argument with a point made in Chapter 1 about the Court's location in political time.

The only sensible first-order rule for Justice X, I believe, is "Do the Right Thing," where the Right Thing in any case is what the justice's combined views about policy and the Constitution commend. Doing the Right Thing in every case would make us better off by the Right Thing's very definition.

The fact that Justice X is a Supreme Court justice makes the story more complicated and drives the justice toward a second-order rule. As a justice she sits at the top of a judicial hierarchy with lots of lower court judges who make lots of decisions about the Constitution. Justice X wouldn't care about what those lower court judges did if she could review every one of their decisions, affirming those that managed to Do the Right Thing and reversing those that didn't. She knows, though, that her time and energy are limited and that she's not going to be able to reverse all the mistaken lower court decisions. What she needs, then, is some way to keep the number of unreviewed mistaken decisions as low as she can (or, put another way, to jack up the number of unreviewed correct decisions).[4]

A constitutional theory of interpretation might fill the bill if it's constructed correctly. Here's how Justice X thinks: Those bozos

---

4. I focus on lower court judges because Justice X can do something about them when they "misbehave"—reverse their decisions. She might want to influence future Supreme Court justices (after she's gone), legal academics, and opinion leaders, but she can't do anything to them if they ignore her.

on the lower courts will go wrong too often if all I tell them is Do the Right Thing because—as ever—they and I might well disagree about what the Right Thing is (and I want *my* vision of the Right Thing to prevail). But, if they follow this theory—originalism, a moral reading of the Constitution, a living Constitution—they won't be able simply to say that the law is what they think the Right Thing is. And I'm going to pick the theory that in the widest range of cases that I can imagine ends up Doing the Right Thing from my point of view. The bozos will still make some mistakes in applying the theory but—if I pick the theory correctly—they'll make fewer mistakes, which is to say, deviate from the Right Thing less often, than they would if I didn't tell them what theory to follow. And, with the number of mistakes down I actually can review and reverse all of them.

This is, as far as I can tell, a perfectly good second-order argument for making us better off from Justice X's point of view. Things are, again as always, more complicated. Justice X knows that sometimes—she hopes not too often—the theory she settles on will require that *she* Do the Wrong Thing (a conservative originalist discovers that originalism leads to a liberal result once in a blue moon). She can't override the theory's implications selectively without muddying the message she's sending to the lower courts. So, every once in a while a conservative originalist will have to cast a liberal vote—or a liberal "living constitutionalist" will have to cast a conservative one. Resisting the temptation to abandon the theory when it leads to inconvenient results is likely to be psychologically difficult. There's now a burgeoning scholarly literature on "selective originalism," for example, which seems empirically well-grounded.[5]

5. This is primarily a problem for judicial originalism (or theory). Academic originalists (and theorists) might not feel the same psychological pressure to bring their policy views into alignment with their theoretical commitments.

Unfortunately, being consistent enough for government work, so to speak, isn't going to accomplish the second-order rule's goal. A lower court judge can point to the Court's selectivity to say to herself, "Sometimes they think that their theory can properly yield to the need to Do the Right Thing. I agree (and so I am faithfully following the theory that they in practice follow), and this is one of those times." And then we're back to the problem posed by a mass of mistaken but effectively unreviewable decisions, which the second-order rule was supposed to solve.

In addition, Justice X's constitutional theory has to leave lower court judges with little room to maneuver—to simplify the point, the constitutional theory has to be reasonably simple. That's why Justice X adopts a single theory rather than a pluralist one with numerous components. Otherwise a lower court judge can tack back and forth among the different components to Do the Right Thing from her point of view.

The same problem arises, though, with a complicated single component theory, whether it be originalism, the moral reading, or living constitutionalism. The next chapter shows that, when you try to work it out in detail, originalism gets pretty complicated, drawing a distinction between interpretation and construction, taking a complicated position on the proper role of wrongly decided precedents, puzzled by problems of conflicting evidence, and more. As scholars who have worked with John Hart Ely's theory of representation reinforcement, discussed in Chapter 2, have shown, the same is true of that theory—and as I'll argue in Chapter 5 of any other candidate for a single-approach constitutional theory.

To do what's required, each specific constitutional theory has to be simple and applied consistently. Now for an additional difficulty. Move from our single Justice X to a multi-member Court, a majority of whose members *broadly* accept one constitutional theory. The odds are quite high that more than occasionally one or more will disagree with the others about what the theory requires in a case before them. That's going to undermine both consistency and simplicity.

For several reasons, then, constitutional theory can't do what judges want from it. But something else, roughly within the same domain, can: If the lower court judges are quite likely to have the same idea of the Right Thing that Justice X does, the justice can follow the "Do the Right Thing" rule, tell the lower court judges to do the same, and watch them do pretty much what Justice X would do herself (and the number of cases that Justice X will have to review to get the right answer will drop to a manageable level). We saw in Chapter 1 that this happens when there's a stable constitutional regime in place. Again roughly speaking, presidents will have nominated enough Supreme Court justices and lower court judges to ensure (with some deviations, of course) that they all think the same way.

Here's one clue to the modern rise of constitutional theory. It began when the New Deal/Great Society order was in decline, wasn't all that important during the Reagan Revolution era, and rose to prominence again as that order declined. And it's taken on its current importance because lower court judges aren't yet in alignment with the current Supreme Court majority (or maybe better, haven't yet come into alignment with it).[6]

Is there some alternative to constitutional theory suitable for the current period and periods of stable constitutional orders? Put another way, what do judges do during such stable periods when they don't need constitutional theory?

---

6. This can't be the full story about the rise of constitutional theory because it wasn't prominent, indeed probably didn't even exist in a currently recognizable form, in earlier periods of transitions between constitutional orders. One suggestion I've heard is that the extra ingredient in the late twentieth century was the development of a serious practice of academic law.

REASONED JUDGMENT AS AN
ALTERNATIVE TO CONSTITUTIONAL THEORY

An opinion in the now-overruled abortion decision *Casey v. Planned Parenthood of Southeastern Pennsylvania* has this statement, probably written by Justice David Souter: "The inescapable fact is that adjudication . . . may call upon the Court in interpreting the Constitution to exercise that same capacity which by tradition courts have always exercised: reasoned judgment. Its boundaries are not susceptible of expression as a simple rule."

Justice Scalia's dissent in the same case included several pages discussing lines from that same opinion that he quoted in bold-faced type and called "outrageous." The reference to "reasoned judgment" was the very first outrageous statement he identified: "'reasoned judgment' . . . turns out to be nothing but philosophical predilection and moral intuition."

In referring to "predilection" Justice Scalia evokes the problem that constitutionalism was supposed to solve, the fact that we disagree among ourselves about the Right Thing to Do. The problem underlying constitutionalism does indeed rule out the possibility that the institutional settlement that constitutionalism seeks to achieve could rest upon purely personal judgments about the Right and the Good. And the fact of reasonable disagreement about the Right and the Good also rules out the possibility that the institutional settlement can rest upon what's really Right and Good.

The *Casey* opinion's reference to judicial "tradition" provides a hint of what I believe is a real alternative to the merely personal and the really true. In 1981, Harvard law professor Charles Fried reminded readers of a phrase used by the British jurist Lord Coke in connection with the common law of contracts and torts. Coke referred to "the artificial Reason" of the law, which was, according to Fried, what lawyers knew. Fried framed his discussion with discussions of the then-increasing influence of the economic analysis of law (associated with Richard Posner, whom we've already encountered)—a theory about the common law. The law's artificial reason, for Fried, was the real world counter to the economic analysis of law and, Fried continued, to the direct application of moral philosophy to the law.

For our purposes the important feature of law's artificial reason is its complexity and, as Fried puts it, its "lumpiness." The common law just can't be simplified to the point where theory is helpful. I believe that Fried's argument is equally applicable to constitutional theory. It can't capture what lawyers and judges know.

Yet, using their knowledge, lawyers make arguments and judges make decisions every day. Without theory how can they do that? Fried argues that they work out the meaning of specifically legal concepts as they confront one case after another. The law's artificial reason is exhibited in, or perhaps even identified with, the modes of argument lawyers deploy.

For myself, I'd put the point a bit differently, though in the end I think my version and Fried's might not be all that different. Lawyers and judges work with a large body of materials—texts (the Constitution and statutes), previously decided cases that seem relevant but also distinguishable (the precedents), and, importantly for present purposes, the ideas and intuitions captured in all the constitutional theories that are rattling around at any time.

Instead of using those theories directly, though, lawyers and judges construct smaller versions: instead of an originalist or moral reading of the First Amendment, an account—call it a theory if you want—about what sorts of regulations of commercial speech, of sexually explicit speech, of hate speech, and of political speech are allowed or banned by the amendment. (If the syntax isn't entirely clear, that's four small theories, not one large one.) Those theories are going to have some points of contact with each other, but lawyers and judges will explain why the small theory of hate speech is different from the small theory of commercial speech.

Confronted with a new case (which is to say, confronted with a case), lawyers and judges sometimes experience it as something like an irritant or an itch. Sure, the available materials might seem to point pretty clearly to a particular result in the case but that result seems a bit off or unsatisfying. They look at all the available legal materials to see if they can figure out whether something in them—sometimes explicitly noted, sometimes to be teased out of the facts and the way earlier lawyers and judges have talked about the problem—explains how to live with the itch or how to get rid of it. They've developed a number of techniques for doing that and developing arguments aimed at leading readers to accept the outcomes—again, to live with the itch because we can't do better, or get rid of it by stating a new legal rule consistent with the existing materials—as at least defensible even if they differ from what the readers would prefer. We can, if we want to, call these techniques a pluralist or eclectic constitutional theory, but I'll suggest in Chapter 5 that we'd be well advised not to.

What lawyers know are these techniques. What they do is use them. When they use them well the results will be acceptable even to those who disagree about what's the Right Thing to Do. Using them well means that the judge has good judgment—or, to revert to the *Casey* opinion, is exercising reasoned judgment. Good lawyering, that is, is a key component to the institutional settlement that's designed to let people with fundamental differences about good public policy continue to live together. Or at least that's the hope.

Two questions (maybe more, but these are the ones that I think matter) remain. First, is the artificial reason of the law better than every candidate constitutional theory? My argument that constitutional theory can't do what's asked of it suggests that the answer here is Yes, though of course I couldn't reasonably contend that

I've conclusively shown that. To do so, I suspect, I'd have to somehow give you a deep understanding of law's artificial reason by deploying the lawyers' techniques in one case after another—in short, by giving you a solid legal education.

Second, can we identify good lawyering? The material in Chapters 1 and 2 suggests that we can. Maybe Potter Stewart's observation about hard-core pornography is applicable here: We know good lawyering when we see it—or at least we know enough to be able to say that Potter Stewart was a merely competent judge and Oliver Wendell Holmes a great one.

Yet, as the feminist legal scholar Catharine MacKinnon observed about pornography, what Stewart saw when he looked at sexually explicit material wasn't what MacKinnon saw. Her point was that "seeing" of that sort is a socially embedded practice. So too with good lawyering. As social conditions change, so will what we see as good lawyering. In the Conclusion I offer some observations about the historical and social construction of understandings of good lawyering.

WHY GOOD JUDGMENT ISN'T
A CONSTITUTIONAL THEORY
(AND WHY THAT MATTERS)

In a work published in 2023, Harvard law professor Cass Sunstein sought "to ask and answer a single question: How should we choose a theory of constitutional interpretation?"[7] He offered a "simple answer: Judges (and others) should choose the theory that would make the American constitutional order better rather than worse."

Sunstein's presentation rather strongly suggests the following

---

7. Here he repeated a question asked a few decades earlier by his colleague Richard Fallon.

process: First identify outcomes that would make the constitutional order better rather than worse, then look around for—or construct—a constitutional theory that, on net, generates more of those outcomes than any other theory, and (of course) choose that theory. This is unpromising on one familiar ground and on a second to be examined in this section.

The familiar ground is that in a world where people disagree about what outcomes make the constitutional order better and worse, the search for or construction of a theory won't do anything in the way of an institutional settlement that will let us live together notwithstanding our disagreements. The disagreements will simply be reproduced at the level of theory.

The new ground is this: Good judges—the people we met in Chapters 1 and 2 and that I discussed in the previous section of this chapter—don't *choose* theories and then apply them. They make decisions and then, sometimes, someone else comes along—these days, a legal academic—and redescribes the decisions as applications of constitutional theory.

Drawing upon what are known as the "theory wars" in literary criticism, the literary scholar and quondam law professor Stanley Fish made the argument elegantly shortly after constitutional theory had gained a foothold in the legal academy. Fish's article began by quoting an exchange between a sports writer and Dennis Martinez, then pitching for the Baltimore Orioles. The writer asked Martinez what he and his manager talked about during an exchange the writer had observed. Martinez replied that the manager said, "Throw strikes and keep 'em off the bases." Martinez replied "O.K.," then continued, "What else could I say? What else could he say?"[8]

---

8. Fish mistakenly disparaged Martinez's talents, writing that Martinez was "unlikely ever to make it into the Baseball Hall of Fame." A few years later

Fish called Martinez's final observation "brilliant." The writer, he suggested, expected Martinez to say that the manager had given him "some set of directions or an articulated method, . . . which Martinez could first grasp . . . and then consult" as needed. Instead, the manager "simply . . . reminde[d] [Martinez of] something that Martinez must surely already know." Fish read the episode as one in which the sports writer was looking for a theory that guided Martinez's actions and Martinez observed that he didn't follow theories but merely tried to perform the acts that the game's rules called for (for pitchers, keeping hitters from reaching the bases). He re-characterized Martinez's response:

> Look, it may be your job to characterize the game of baseball in terms of overriding theories, but it's my job to play it; and playing has nothing to do with following words of wisdom . . . and everything to do with already being someone whose sense of himself and his possible actions is inseparable from the kind of knowledge that words of wisdom would presume to impart.

Martinez, we might say, understood the Nike slogan before it became popular: "Just do it."

Transfer this account to law. Baseball is a practice that its players engage in having assimilated into their very beings rules and strategies that vary as circumstances change: Infielders know—without saying anything to themselves about why—how much to shift to the right or left when a batter approaches the plate and takes his stance. So too with good lawyers: They operate within a field defined by rules but the most interesting of those rules don't have a precise content independent of the circumstances. The

---

Martinez pitched a perfect game, he appeared in four All-Star Games, and was inducted into the Canadian Baseball Hall of Fame.

range of possible meanings might be narrow or broad (it would be rare, though probably not unheard of, for a shortstop to move outside the third-base foul line). Good lawyers "simply" know what to do. Fish did leave some room for theory—as part of a *different* practice: Not the practice of deciding cases or arguing for clients' positions but the practice of some legal academics.

Good lawyers' knowledge comes from somewhere, of course. It doesn't come from theory, though. Rather, it comes from the experiences they have had in working with the law over their careers—what Fish calls the "knowledge that develops in the trial-and-error attempt to match an example." Part but only part of those experiences consists of thinking theoretically: "talking theory is one of the resources [the good lawyer] employs in the course of [getting something done]," as Fish puts it. And, as I'll argue in the Conclusion, sometimes that resource plays smaller, sometimes larger roles in the practice.

The legal theorist Karl Llewellyn described good decisions by judges as following "the law of the singing reason." My students once accurately described what Llewellyn had in mind as something akin to the experience of hearing a heavenly choir burst out when the judge gets it right. Notably, Llewellyn supported his argument with a list of lawyers and judges who knew when the choir appeared on the scene.

The mere fact of the list points to another important component of the argument against theory. Skeptical readers might think that relying on the law of the singing reason is unduly subjective: I might hear the choir singing, you might hear nothing at all, or mere noise. And, as ever, the concern about subjectivity is that it allows judges to impose as law whatever they personally think best (again, the Right Thing as they—but not others—see it).

Like the list of great judges presented in Chapter 1, Llewellyn's list of good lawyers suggests a possible route away from subjectivity. Good lawyers are people whose capacity to exercise good judgment is validated by the community of lawyers within which they operate. Recall that the list of great judges didn't result from giving a bunch of people a checklist of characteristics that make a judge great (Fish's "words of wisdom"). Asking survey respondents to list "great" judges without giving them theoretical guidance elicits judgments that are overall untheorized even when some respondents do deploy their preferred theoretical perspective to come up with their personal lists.

And now a final point about *judging* as a practice. We have to consider the possibility that lists of great judges will be sensitive to the composition of the survey population. To adapt a question posed in one of the central works of U.S. legal theory of the 1950s, do we think that the board of directors of the U.S. Chamber of Commerce would come up with the same list as the Central Committee of the Chinese Communist Party? That those attending the Republican party's national convention in 2024 would come up with the same list as those attending the Democratic party's convention?

And yet: Suppose that in attempt to cleanse the responses of immediate political controversies we told the survey respondents that they couldn't put on the list anyone who sat on the Supreme Court after 2000? Now are you confident that the lists would be all that different?

Shift now from the judges' and lawyers' perspectives to the citizens'. The people in the stands when Martinez and his manager invoked the practice of pitching aren't playing baseball. They're watching it. That too, though, is a practice. To use terms familiar from political theory, they've chosen to go to a baseball game and in doing so they've bought into whatever that entails. We could change our minds. We could eventually come to think that soccer or cricket is our national sport—that we should treat the Constitution as a recommendation. Again that's part of what regime shifts sometimes produce. But for us, today, we've chosen to treat the Constitution as binding law, which means, as Fish and Fried would have it, that we've bought into the idea that judging involves lawyering, not constitutional theory.

Before exploring these last matters in the Conclusion, generalized into questions about the social construction of the idea of good judgment, I turn to other ways of contrasting theory with practice.

CHAPTER 4

Why It's a Mistake to Ask
Whether Originalism Is a Good
Constitutional Theory

If you've picked this book up, you already know that originalism is a theory about how judges should interpret the Constitution. A simple definition—things will get more complicated soon—is that originalism requires that judges interpret the Constitution according to the public understandings of its terms' meanings when those terms were written (1789 for the original Constitution, 1791 for the Bill of Rights, and 1868 for the Fourteenth Amendment). You also know that a majority of today's Supreme Court justices say that they are originalists. That's given originalism a conservative ideological cast, though in principle we could have a progressive originalist Constitution (if that's what its words were understood to mean when they were adopted).

There's a cottage industry among liberals and progressives attacking originalism as a constitutional theory. Writing a long-form opinion piece in the *Washington Post,* Ruth Marcus says that "originalism is bunk." Dean Erwin Chemerinsky writes that originalism is "worse than nothing"—that is, we'd be better off if the justices had *no* theory of constitutional interpretation instead of being originalists. Harvard law professor Cass Sunstein advises readers about "how to interpret the Constitution," with the clear though not openly stated message that originalism isn't a good choice.

The chapter titles in Dean Chemerinsky's book tell us what the usual liberal criticisms of originalism are:

- "epistemological"—we can't know in general what the original understandings were (and though we might know what some individuals believed some specific terms meant we can't aggregate those individual understandings into a more general shared understanding—more on this below);
- "abhorrence"—sometimes we can know what the original understandings were, and they imply that some policies that legislatures have in fact adopted are, well, abhorrent, with slavery and racial segregation being the primary examples;
- "modernity"—originalists have no good account of how to apply understandings from 1789 and 1868 to practices unknown and unanticipatable then (and when they try to supply an account they come up with distinctions that non-originalists love to use); liberals often refer here to technologies like monitoring of individuals' social media accounts (and semiautomatic weapons), which are met by originalist invocations of underlying principles of privacy (and free expression and equality in other examples) that were said to be part of the original understanding;
- "hypocrisy"—in practice originalist judges are selective in their originalism, using it when they're presented with information about original understandings that fits their existing conservative beliefs and abandoning it when they can't find information about original understandings that supports those beliefs or, worse, when the originalist material actually points against those beliefs (here the primary example liberals use is race-based affirmative action, but free expression is another).

This book isn't another compendium of criticisms of originalism, though in the course of this chapter I'll develop a few that contribute to the exposition of my main theme. Rather, it's an argument that the entire enterprise of trying to come up with a master constitutional theory of interpretation is misconceived. To adapt Dean Chemerinsky's phrase, originalism isn't the only theory worse than nothing; all theories are. We would do better, and indeed have done better in the past, by abandoning the effort to "choose a constitutional theory" as Sunstein asks, and asking instead that our judges exercise "reasoned judgment."

Here's a clue to the reason for that request: Anyone who gets into the details of originalist constitutional theory discovers something reasonably quickly—that there are really *two* kinds of originalist theory. There's originalism as developed in the legal academy (which has numerous variants but some central tendencies) and then there's originalism as practiced by judges and defended by conservative op-ed writers. Academic originalism is often quite sophisticated—sometimes, in my view, too sophisticated in its effort to appropriate for legal analysis concepts developed by philosophers of language to deal with an entirely different set of problems (and sometimes not well understood by the law professors who appropriate the concepts). Academic originalism has come up with decent responses to many of the critiques offered by progressives and liberals. They handle simple versions of Chemerinsky's "epistemological" concerns reasonably well, though as I'll argue they have trouble with more complicated— and better—versions. Similarly with the "modernity" problem.

Academic originalism might offer a coherent account of constitutional interpretation, or at least an account as coherent as any other. Liberal academic criticisms and liberal op-ed articles can't drive a stake through its heart. Academic originalism's difficulties are two. The less important is that the coherent account has quite a few bells and whistles added to the initial account, designed to address the progressive and liberal critiques. For an academic enterprise that's no big deal. As Albert Einstein is said to have said,

"Everything should be made as simple as possible, but no simpler." If the best account of a theory of original understanding is complicated, so be it.

The more important difficulty with academic originalism is that, probably precisely because it's become more complicated so that it can deal with objections, it's become increasingly remote from actual judicial practice, in part because judges need simple, usable theories. Judicial practitioners of originalism and their acolytes on the op-ed pages continue to defend originalism on grounds that "ordinary" readers—people like those to whom this book is directed—can readily grasp. And they rely on *those* grounds not simply to defend originalism as a theory of interpretation but to defend the specific results they reach in their decisions. Sometimes in doing so the judges and, more often, the op-ed writers point to academic originalism to rebut criticisms, without recognizing that the distinctions drawn by academic originalists actually undermine the results they're trying to defend.

I've said that the distinction between academic and judicial originalism offers a clue to why the enterprise of looking for a theory of interpretation is misconceived. The next section of this chapter pursues that clue by elaborating some of the progressive and liberal criticisms already mentioned. The "reveal" at the end of the story is this: Constitutional interpretation is a *practical* enterprise not a theoretical one, and it can only be understood by examining and attempting to "get inside" the practice by seeing what actually happens when judges interpret the Constitution. Academics have constitutional theories. Judges make decisions.

PUTTING ONE RED HERRING ASIDE: ORIGINALISM ISN'T "REAL" HISTORY BUT THAT DOESN'T MATTER

Most academic historians bridle at the historical work that passes for originalism, and not merely because most academic historians are liberals and most originalists are conservatives. Academic historians have a well-established technique for figuring out how people in the past understood ideas about governing. As the most prominent school of thought puts it, they look at ideas in context. To understand how people in the framing generation thought about the right to keep and bear arms, for example, they'd start with ideas about governing generally—who has power, where that power comes from (and in particular the connection between earthly power and Christianity), and other ideas operating on a fairly high level of generality about how society is organized. Then they'd work downward—and almost always they'd discover enormous interconnected ambiguities.

Thomas Jefferson observed in 1816 that the framing period was very much like the present but without forty years of experience.[1] More than two hundred years later we aren't "very much like" the people of 1789. True, we, like they, respond to incentives, are simultaneously somewhat self-interested and somewhat public-regarding. Yet they, unlike we, lived in a world in which religion was pervasively present for everyone (and religion generally meant Christianity in several variants, some of which were more tolerant of other religions than others); they unlike we lived in a world in which the idea that sovereignty—earthly power—was lodged in a single monarch was a real possibility; and of course much more.

After some floundering, academic originalists settled on a

---

1. His observation is so eloquent that it deserves quoting in full: "Some men look at Constitutions with sanctimonious reverence, & deem them, like the ark of the covenant, too sacred to be touched. they ascribe to the men of the preceding age a wisdom more than human, and suppose what they did to be beyond amendment. I knew that age well: I belonged to it, and labored with it. it deserved well of it's country. it was very like the present, but without the experience of the present: and 40. years of experience in government is worth a century of book-reading: and this they would say themselves, were they to rise from the dead."

response. We have to understand history-as-practiced-by-origi-nalists as categorically different from history-as-practiced-by-historians. It's not that the former is good enough for government work, so to speak: the best you can expect lawyers and judges to do when they try to do "real" history. Rather, the point is that history as practiced by originalists is a *legal* practice to be evaluated according to criteria drawn from law not academic history. As we saw in Chapter 3, the legal criteria for constitutional theory are simplicity and consistency. How does originalism fare according to those criteria?

SOME PROBLEMS WITH ORIGINALISM THAT HELP US UNDERSTAND WHY INTERPRETATION ISN'T A THEORETICAL ACTIVITY

Modern originalism has a well-known political and intellectual history. It began as an effort to come up with some way of explaining to the public why the Warren Court's liberal decisions were wrong. Conservatives settled on originalism as their weapon of choice: The decisions they criticized were wrong not because they were inconsistent with party-political commitments (that was obviously unpromising as a line of attack), or because they were inconsistent with some widely agreed upon moral or political theory (they were inconsistent with *some* moral and political theories but not with equally respectable others) but because they couldn't be rooted in something about the original Constitution.

Initially that "something" was the intentions of the Constitution's framers. This jurisprudence of original intention, as Attorney General Edwin Meese called it, came under sustained and successful attack, mostly for the epistemological reasons I've already sketched: You couldn't know enough about the intentions of enough of the framers to draw confident conclusions about "their" intentions. And, even worse, you couldn't figure out how to add the intentions of individuals together to come up with original intentions with respect to specific provisions.[2]

Originalism was then reformulated as a jurisprudence of original public understandings or original public meaning. "Public" helped because it got away from the difficulties associated with trying to figure out and then add together what was going on in people's heads. And you could find evidence of original public meaning by looking at how people in 1789 or 1868 used the words they put into the Constitution *in other contexts.*

So, originalism—at least academic originalism—improved. It still had problems, though.

Original expected applications. How could the framing generation possibly have understood the phrase "cruel and unusual punishments" to license courts to find the death penalty unconstitutional, when that same generation routinely enacted and enforced capital punishment? More pointedly, how could the public in 1868 have understood the Fourteenth Amendment to mean that racially segregated schools were now constitutionally prohibited, when legislatures at the time and thereafter enacted statutes requiring racially segregated schools?

These are questions about the "original expected applications" of constitutional terms, an approach we encountered in Chapter 2's discussion of the Blaisdell case. Contemporary originalism has a number of responses, aimed almost specifically though often implicitly at showing that *Brown v. Board of Education,* finding racial segregation in schools unconstitutional, could have rested on originalist grounds.

2. There's a dense philosophical literature about what we mean when we talk about individuals acting together, but originalist theorists never tried to invoke it for their purposes, and in my view properly so: That literature wouldn't help with the problems of interpretation they worried about.

Response 1. Maybe the Eighth Amendment's ban on cruel and unusual punishments invalidates punishments that are *truly* cruel and unusual. Maybe in 1791 capital punishment wasn't unusual, for example, but the word "unusual" might have been understood to mean "unusual at the time decisions are being made." Similarly with cruelty: The framing generation might have understood that notions of what's cruel change (they'd experienced such changes in their lifetimes, perhaps), and understood that they wrote a provision that would require later generations to ask, "Do we think that capital punishment is cruel *now?*"

A similar argument might be made about school segregation. The Fourteenth Amendment might have been understood to enact a requirement of equality—*real* equality. The framing generation might have mistakenly believed that racial segregation could be equal. Or, perhaps most people actually understood it to violate the constitutional requirement of equality but succumbed to immediate political pressures and enacted statutes that they understood to be inconsistent with the Fourteenth Amendment.[3]

---

3. I've written here of "the Fourteenth Amendment" in general without identifying any specific provision in that amendment. For many generations the idea that the Fourteenth Amendment guaranteed equality was located in the provision saying that no state may deny "the equal protection of the laws." Originalist arguments going back quite a ways question that location. The catch phrase is that the equal protection clause guarantees that whatever laws there are will be enforced equally but doesn't guarantee the protection of equal laws, that is, laws that treat everyone the same. Originalists today are searching for other places to locate the amendment's guarantee of equality, with some focusing on the provision that states can't deny "privileges or immunities of citizens of the United States," which isn't all that promising because the term "privileges or immunities" doesn't appear to say anything about equality. More promising is the idea that the Fourteenth Amendment's references to citizenship are predicated upon the idea that all citizens are equal with respect to civic life. Justice Thomas has suggested that possibility, as have a handful of aca-

Response 2. Originalist scholar and former federal judge Michael McConnell came up with an ingenious argument about the original expected application of the Fourteenth Amendment to racially segregated schools. McConnell observed that quite a few of the people in Congress who voted for the Fourteenth Amendment remained there in later years, when Congress took up proposals to ban racially segregated schools. He looked at how those people voted on those proposals and found that everyone who had voted for the Fourteenth Amendment voted to ban school segregation, and did so, as they said, because in their view the Fourteenth Amendment *required* it.[4] So, McConnell concludes, the Fourteenth Amendment's supporters actually did understand the amendment to ban racially segregated schools.

There's a lot that could be said about this argument. It seems to be a form of original intentions originalism, for example. It's not clear that we should infer from the intentions of the relatively small number of people McConnell's argument identifies—remember, members of Congress who voted both *for* the Fourteenth Amendment *and* to outlaw racially segregated schools—that the amendment's *public* meaning was the one McConnell describes. That's especially true when there's a time gap between the date of the amendment's adoption and the dates of the congressional votes to ban school segregation.

McConnell's argument doesn't fit well into the best contemporary versions of originalism. There's no High Court of Originalism, of course, and he's as entitled as anyone else to come up with a version of originalism that he's comfortable with. But we

---

demic articles, but the originalist spadework hasn't yet been done to establish this proposition.

4. McConnell argues that the proposals weren't adopted because of contingent political circumstances that prevented the House and Senate from coming to agreement on a single proposal within a single congressional term.

should note one additional point: Other originalists, who hold more standard versions of originalism, routinely cite McConnell's article to show that *Brown v. Board of Education* is consistent with the original understanding of the Fourteenth Amendment without attempting to reconcile McConnell's somewhat idiosyncratic version of originalism with their own.[5] This is a scholarly phenomenon—I call it the "one and done" approach—that we'll see again: Once some originalist has come up with an argument that originalism isn't abhorrent (because it actually doesn't allow racial segregation), other originalists don't revisit the question.

Response 3. The best among today's originalists say that original expected applications are relevant to determining original public meaning but not conclusive. They're relevant because we ordinarily can use the way people act when guided or constrained by some rule as an indication of what they believe the rule to mean. They're not conclusive in part because we might find other evidence of public meaning that's inconsistent with the inferences about meaning we draw from behavior. And, probably more important, they're not conclusive because sometimes we can explain their apparent deviation from the rule's public meaning by referring to immediate political pressures, which serve here as before as an explanation that allows us to set aside their behavior as a guide to public meaning.

Liquidation and the construction zone. Some constitutional provisions are pretty specific. Nobody's going to give you much of an argument about the proposition that Representative Maxwell Frost, born in 1997, isn't eligible for the presidency in 2024 or 2028 because he won't be thirty-five years old then. Other provisions are rather abstract: Congress can make no law abridging the free-

---

5. Sometimes these citations are a bit cautious, introduced with phrases akin to, "For an originalist argument for *Brown*, see McConnell," or the more arcane but equivalent "Cf. McConnell."

dom of speech, but what's the freedom of speech and what counts as an abridgement of it? Originalists deal with the relatively abstract provisions in several ways.

1. *What the abstract provision* really *means.* I've already mentioned one possibility. The original public meaning of "the freedom of speech" was the freedom of speech as it is best understood. People knew that their current understanding of what that was might be flawed and knew as well that understandings might change—and, they hoped, improve. The original public meaning of "the freedom of speech," then, is "the best extant understanding of the freedom of speech at the time an issue about its meaning arises."

Consider here how the prevailing opinion in the now-overruled abortion decision *Casey v. Planned Parenthood* explained why two important precedents were wrongly decided. *Plessy v. Ferguson* held that states could require racial segregation if the facilities available to both races were separate but equal. *Casey* said that this was wrong because the factual assumption that separate facilities could be equal was mistaken, probably at the time *Plessy* was decided and certainly by the time it was overruled. *Lochner v. New York* struck down a statute saying that bakers couldn't work more than ten hours a day. *Casey* said that the decision was wrong because the Court mistakenly believed that individual bakers and their employers were in a position to strike fair bargains.[6] I think that many scholars think these distinctions are disingenuous because the real reason the decisions were wrong ran much deeper than factual error, but *Casey*'s analysis illustrates how "real" meanings can be mistakenly displaced.

Notably this approach to giving abstract terms meaning is pretty much what advocates of a "living constitution" would say.

---

6. On *Casey*'s account the state legislature made the factual mistake in *Plessy*, whereas the Court made the factual mistake in *Lochner*.

It's similar, maybe even identical to the distinction the legal philosopher and originalism critic Ronald Dworkin drew between general concepts and specific and possibly flawed conceptions of those concepts. To switch the example to another abstract term or idea—equality—Justice William O. Douglas, no originalist, once justified a decision by writing, "Notions of what constitutes equal treatment for purposes of the Equal Protection Clause do change."

2. *Liquidation (mostly by legislatures)*. Writing in *The Federalist Papers* number 37, James Madison observed, "All new laws . . . are considered as more or less obscure and equivocal, until their meaning be liquidated and ascertained by a series of particular discussions and adjudications." An obscure or equivocal term gets its meaning over time as legislatures enact statutes reflecting the legislative understanding of the term's meaning. Congress might immunize some speech from regulation or, more likely, subject it to regulation, thereby indicating what its members understood "the freedom of expression" to mean. This approach runs the risk of leading to the conclusion, "Whatever is, is constitutionally permissible." Any new statute restricting freedom of speech—a campaign finance law or a law banning exceptionally gross depictions of cruelty to animals—is just another step toward the liquidation of the First Amendment's meaning. We can avoid the difficulty by saying that enough time has passed for the term's meaning to have been completely liquidated. Some originalists have tried to avoid this conclusion by developing criteria for determining what should count toward liquidating meaning. The effort is at present in its early stages and it might not settle into originalism's structure.

3. *Construction (mostly by courts)*. Madison referred to "adjudications." Many contemporary originalists accept the proposition that many constitutional provisions require "construction" in the courts. They refer to a "construction zone" in which courts "build out" the provision's meaning, developing more specific meanings

consistent with what the (rather abstract) provision was understood to mean when it was adopted. Depending on how expansively we think courts can construe constitutional terms—how large the construction zone is—and, importantly, how many and which provisions are subject to construction, this version of originalism, like the "real meaning" version, converges with non-originalist reliance on general principles of good governance.

Contested original public meanings. What if investigation into original public meaning seems to show that the original public meaning of some provision was contested? I call this the "60/40" (or "70/30") problem: You look at the relevant materials and discover that 60 or 70 percent of them seem to reflect one understanding, 40 or 30 percent another. Here are three examples.

1. *The First Amendment.* My perhaps singular view is that there are two decent candidates for the original public meaning of "freedom of speech" and "abridgement." According to one candidate view, you could say anything you wanted at the risk of later being held liable for inflicting injury on other people or violating good morals or disrupting the public order. This—especially the "good morals" and "public order" limits—would license legislatures to adopt a rather wide range of restrictions on free speech. According to the other, you could say anything you wanted at the risk of later being held liable for libel, blasphemy, obscenity, and a handful of other offenses. Here the general principle of free speech was understood to be subject to only a limited and short list of exceptions.

2. *The "commerce" clause.* The Constitution gives Congress the power to regulate "Commerce among the several States." Does "commerce" include manufacturing? Scholars who have examined what people in 1789 understood by the word "commerce" have come up with two possibilities. One, endorsed by Chief Justice John Marshall in 1824, is that the term refers to "commercial intercourse . . . in all its branches." On this view manufacturing

is indeed commerce. The other rejects that conclusion, observing that you can find lots of phrases akin to "agriculture, manufacturing, and commerce," which of course implies that commerce is something different from manufacturing.

3. *The "nondelegation" doctrine.* Everyone agrees that the president can't make rules for the entire country on his or her own. Everyone also agrees that Congress can authorize the president to make *some* rules of that sort. Are there limits to this power of Congress to "delegate" rule-making authority to the president? Scholars who have examined the relevant materials have discovered a structure quite similar to the one I described for the First Amendment. I simplify the scholarship to make its conclusions easier to understand, but without, I believe, distorting it. On one view Congress's power to delegate was limited to what's become known as "filling in the details" of statutes where Congress identified a reasonably specific set of guiding principles, with some limited exceptions for broader delegations in areas of especially important national concern. On the other view the so-called exceptions actually stand for the proposition that Congress's power to delegate was unlimited.

Sometimes originalists deny that 60/40 problems actually arise (with respect to provisions that are of interest today). Liquidation and construction might deal with some contested meanings, though originalist scholarship doesn't seem to have focused on that possibility. More commonly the scholarship denies that there's a 60/40 problem because the materials show overwhelming support for one view (call it a "95/5" situation), with the tiny minority obvious outliers or cranks. The "no problem" position is reinforced by an understandable feature of academic life. Once someone has gone to all the effort of locating the materials (reading through a mound of old documents to isolate the discussion of the provision of interest), no other originalist has much incentive to do it all over again—the "one and done" phenomenon. So, the "no problem" position settles into the scholarship and can then seep into judicial originalist opinions.

There's a lurking difficulty. Assume, as has typically been the case, that the "no problem" law review article supports a conservative-leaning interpretation. Liberals and progressives have caught on to the game and they've started to produce their own originalist scholarship. And *they* have an incentive to convert the 95/5 position into a 60/40 one—as indeed they've begun to. That's not to say that liberal originalism has decisively established *its* claims. Rather, it's put the "60/40" problem back on the table. Here are some possible solutions, two "within" originalism, one outside it.

Solution 1. The original public understanding is a matter of historical fact. We know how to deal with conflicting evidence about historical facts. Did the car involved in a crash run a red light just before the crash? We listen to eyewitnesses, take measurements of skid marks, and the like. Sometimes the evidence is conflicting: One witness says that the light was red, another that it had just turned yellow—but the first one was farther away from the light than the second. We take all the evidence into account and determine what happened on the basis of some standard—in the example, whether the preponderance of the evidence (our 60 percent) supports the conclusion that the light was red.

Why not do the same thing when the evidence about original public meaning is contested? The answer is that there is, as philosophers would say, a fact of the matter about whether the light was red. (After the trial is over, we might discover some closed-circuit TV recordings showing that the light was yellow, for example.) There's no similar fact of the matter about original public understanding. (There's no equivalent to the CCTV evidence about the stop light.) If we could reanimate everyone from the framing era and ask them what the term in question meant, all we'd get is the same 60/40 division we found from the evidence we had.

Maybe so, an originalist might respond, but as an originalist I have to have *some* way to deal with the 60/40 problem. Something like a preponderance of the evidence standard gives me an answer. True enough, but it's not the only possible answer.

Solution 2. You could say that in a 60/40 situation we ought to specify the meaning to be used in contemporary constitutional interpretation as the meaning that leaves the broadest scope for democratic self-governance. Sometimes that will be the meaning supported by "only" 40 percent of the evidence. The originalist justification for going with that meaning is straightforward: The framing generations were committed to democratic self-governance rather broadly, and resolving the 60/40 problem by going with democratic self-governance is compatible with their overall constitutional vision.

I think it's worth noting that this solution has no obvious contemporary political valence. When the 60/40 problem arises the solution supports today's policy choices. If there's a 60/40 problem about the First Amendment, for example, the solution would allow legislatures to regulate campaign finance *and* to limit the teaching of critical race theory in public schools.

(Non)solution 3. Maybe a single constitutional theory doesn't have to solve every possible problem that critics suggest falls within its domain. If that's right, an originalist could say that 60/40 problems have to be resolved by something other than originalism: political theory or moral philosophy, contemporary judgments about good governance, whatever. This does introduce some pluralism into constitutional theory, but only when 60/40 problems arise. Of course if they arise frequently—if it's not true that the evidence for a singular original meaning is "overwhelming" almost everywhere—the case for a pluralist constitutional theory is going to be strengthened. That's an empirical question but as originalism reaches into more and more areas it seems likely that 60/40 problems will proliferate. My view, again for what it's worth, is that

60/40 problems are already widespread enough to make pluralism a more attractive theory than originalism.

The allure of corpus linguistics. Big Data has come to constitutional interpretation. The form is what's known as "corpus linguistics." Remember that we figure out original understandings or meanings of terms used in the Constitution by looking at the way those terms were used in other contexts. Corpus linguistics begins by compiling a large data base of texts from the period we're interested in. The texts include newspapers, books, dictionaries, legislative debates—anything, really, that can be scanned into some computer-searchable form. Then you submit queries to the data base. You're also careful to ask how often terms were associated with ("collocated with" is the technical term) others, to give you some confidence that you're taking the entire context of use into account.

Take the "interstate commerce" example. You ask how often does the word "commerce" appear in phrases that also include "agriculture" and "manufacturing." Then—this is more difficult— you figure out some way to ask how often phrases were used that treated "manufacturing" as a form of "commerce." Then you compare the uses to figure out which meaning was more widely used.

Some originalists are attracted to corpus linguistics because it has a "scientific" and "objective" feel to it, and as we'll see in Chapter 5 scientific precision and objectivity are a couple of reasons for creating constitutional theory. Corpus linguistics runs up against a number of difficulties, though.

One is in principle surmountable. You have to have a data base that contains material that's likely to tell you about the meanings of terms used in the Constitution. I'll call this "legally inflected" data. If your data base is dominated by novels and poems you're probably not going to get much useful information about legally inflected terms. At present the available data bases are fairly thin. One starts in 1810 and runs through the early 2000s. Querying *it* isn't going to tell you anything about meanings as of 1789 or 1791. What about 1868? It turns out that more than half of the data is drawn from novels and popular magazines. Though the data base does include newspapers from the 1860s you're almost certainly going to get distorted answers to queries about legally inflected terms from it. Another data base of "Founding Era American English" is being built. As of 2021 most of the texts came from the records of only six men, though the base has been expanded since then (in 2021, 4 percent came from another compilation, and in 2023 that number was up to 9 percent). Here your queries are going to get better answers about legally inflected terms, but the evidentiary base is thinner than it could be (no more than 2 percent of the texts are newspapers or pamphlets, for example). You'll get information about how some people used the terms but not much information about how ordinary people alert to legal meaning did.

The data bases will surely expand. Other problems with corpus linguistics won't go away, though. As the "commerce" example indicates, it's actually pretty difficult to formulate queries that are going to give useful answers. Sometimes, as in that example, you can do a decent job in designing a query about one of the possible meanings but will find it difficult to do the same for another of the candidate meanings.

It's reasonably well known that it's difficult to formulate the queries in a strictly objective way. Nobody really expects judges to know enough to do a corpus linguistics exercise well. Rather, as Justice Thomas suggested in a related context, they're going to rely on presentations by lawyers in an adversary system. And those lawyers are going to go into the enterprise with some presuppositions that will shape the queries they come up with. You might think that disinterested experts—linguists, historians—might design queries and use corpus linguistics in a purely scholarly and disinterested way, but you'd be wrong. These experts have their presuppositions as well, and their presuppositions aren't completely independent of the hopes they have about what the investigation will show. And often these supposedly neutral experts are "wrangled" sub rosa by the parties themselves.

Here's a more subtle difficulty. Suppose you ask whether a specific phrase or its equivalents turns up in a data base, and the answer you get is, "No," or "Not very often." Does that mean that the original meaning did *not* include that phrase? The best scholarship says that it doesn't. The query probes for something like original expected applications. And, more important, the query may use terms that are the way we *today* attempt to describe a general concept but overlook ways in which the framers described that concept. Skeptical about the modern doctrine that the Fourth Amendment protects "expectations of privacy," for example, Justice Thomas queried a data base for that precise phrase and, turning up nothing, concluded that the ordinary meaning of the Fourth Amendment in 1791 didn't deal with expectations of privacy. That's a pretty obvious error, but judges have committed similar ones that are less obvious.

A related difficulty is the "frequency" fallacy, which is especially likely to crop up in 60/40 (or, again, 70/30) cases. The fallacy is to conclude that the 60 percent captures the "true" original meaning. Studies from corpus linguistics queries conclude that "commerce" didn't include "manufacturing" or "production" because the uses that pretty clearly exclude manufacturing outnumber the ones that pretty clearly include it. Why is this a fallacy? Two advocates for a careful use of corpus linguistics explain that frequency data might tell us what was likely to come to mind first when the term was used but that "first to mind" use might not be the one enacted as law by people who reflected more deliberatively about its meaning. Frequency gives you some clues about ordinary meaning, just as original expected applications do, but not a definitive answer.

I refrain from accumulating additional examples of difficulties with corpus linguistics. I've said enough to support the conclusion that the bottom line on corpus linguistics and originalism is about the same as the one for original expected applications: What you get from your queries might be relevant to determining original public meaning—another piece of evidence—but it's not the end of the inquiry.

It's worth pointing out as well that here too we can see a disconnect between academic and judicial practice. The best academic defenses of legal corpus linguistics are hedged about with qualifications and "best practices" guidelines. Judges who try to use corpus linguistics themselves are unlikely to qualify their conclusions or follow those guidelines. And, once again, relying on presentations by competing experts isn't likely to make things better: Judges will go with the experts for the side they favor going into the analysis or will ignore the experts (and corpus linguistics itself).

The Second Amendment provides a real-world example. *District of Columbia v. Heller,* the Court's decision holding that the Second Amendment protected an individual right to have weapons "in ordinary use" for purposes of self protection, was decided before the rise of legal corpus linguistics studies. Scholars of the Second Amendment have identified three basic possibilities for its original meaning. (1) Some people understood it to mean that individuals could keep and bear arms so that they could band together with like-minded others to resist an oppressive government (this has been labeled the "insurrectionist" view, where the adjective tends to be given a pejorative spin, though in my view it shouldn't be). (2) Others understood it to mean that people could keep and bear arms in connection with their membership in a state-organized militia (the "militia" view). (3) Still others understood it to mean that individuals could keep and bear arms for self protection, mostly against "marauding natives" and wild animals (the "self-protection" view). For what it's worth, my assessment of the evidence scholars have made available is that this is something like a 45 percent (insurrectionist)/30 percent (militia)/25 percent (self-protection) case, although the precise numbers don't matter.

The Court in *Heller* concluded that the original public meaning was the "self-protection" one. After sensibly interpreting the word "arms" to refer to weapons generally, Justice Scalia turned to "keep and bear arms." He treated the two verbs separately. Keeping arms meant individually owning them; bearing arms meaning carrying them about for whatever purposes one had. He acknowledged that there was an "idiomatic" meaning of "bearing arms," referring to military uses. But, he wrote, this idiomatic use "unequivocally" occurred as "bear arms against." With no limiting term, there was "no doubt" that "keep and bear arms" had the "self-protection" public meaning.[7] Justice Scalia's arguments drew upon framing-era (and some post-framing) dictionaries, constitutional provisions, statutes, and a handful of other sources.

Heller was handed down in 2008. Ten years later two scholars, one a well-known conservative, decided to use corpus linguistics to find out the original public meaning of "keep and bear arms." They concluded: "even when we exclude the phrase 'bear arms against,' the overwhelming majority of instances of 'bear arms' was in the military context. Justice Scalia certainly identified instances when the phrase 'bear arms,' absent the preposition 'against,' had a non-military context—but those usages were less common." What about "keep arms"? "[A]bout half referred to keeping arms in the military context, roughly a quarter referred to a private sense

7. Because it has some bearing on the argument I make in the Conclusion, I note that Justice Scalia's opinion not only expresses no doubts whatever about its conclusion but also contains some of his usual sneers at those with whom he disagrees, including a parenthetical swipe at linguistics departments with the one-word sentence "Grotesque."

of keeping arms, and another quarter or so were ambiguous references." Note of course that the authors here commit the "frequency fallacy." In a follow-up article the authors concluded that Justice Scalia (and Justice Stevens writing in dissent) "should have expressed far more caution when reaching their textualist conclusions based on the narrow subset of founding-era sources they reviewed."

Linguists also weighed in. An amicus brief filed in a follow-up case, *New York State Rifle & Pistol Association v. Bruen*, decided in 2020, summarized corpus linguistics research on the Second Amendment in a section headed "Recent Corpus Linguistics Research Indicates That the Original Common Meaning of 'Bear Arms' and 'Keep Arms' Was Collective and Militaristic." In the "Framing Era" data base, "Out of nearly 1,000 examined uses of 'bear arms' . . . roughly 900 separate occurrences . . . refer to war, soldiering, or other forms of armed action by a group rather than an individual." And "only a handful" of uses "were either ambiguous or carried no military connotation." The linguists reached the same conclusion about "keep arms": Twenty-five of twenty-eight references (a small number, but more than Justice Scalia had found) "refer to weapons for use in the military or the militia."

What did the Court do when presented with this evidence about original meaning? Essentially, nothing. *Bruen* started with the assumption that *Heller* was binding precedent and developed what the Court's majority believed to be the best doctrinal implementation of that precedent.

Suppose, though, that the justices acknowledged that they'd made a mistake in *Heller*. Then another problem arises.

• *The problem of precedent.* As the next chapter describes in more detail, originalism has a long history but has become a dominant constitutional theory only in the past decade. That means that a couple of centuries of cases weren't decided according to originalism alone. Of course some or many results from the past might be defensible in originalist terms. But, not surprisingly, originalists have questioned quite a few older decisions. Two originalists, for example, write that they "doubt the pedigree" of a list of eleven cases, some quite important (and two of which came up in Chapter 2).

Pretty much everyone has an account of when you can and should overrule precedents. Is the wrong decision important or minor? (As it's sometimes put, sometimes it's more important that a legal issue be settled than that it be settled correctly.) Was the wrong decision a close one not in terms of votes on the Court but in terms of the analysis offered for the result? Have people relied on the decision by taking actions that can't be unwound? Here my question is specific to originalism. Does *it* have anything distinctive to say about old decisions that can't be defended on originalist grounds?

For academic originalists the answer might well be, "No." They are responsible to nothing but the truth. Judicial originalists are in a different position. They have to worry about the effects of their decisions. *Fiat justicia ruat caelum* (let justice be done though the heavens fall) is sometimes the right thing to do, but not always. Suppose, as might well be the case, that the original public meaning of the constitutional provision giving Congress the power "to coin Money" was that Congress could create a currency consisting of metal coins but not paper money. The Court decided otherwise in 1871, and holding paper currency unconstitutional today would wreak havoc with the nation's and the world's economy. Justice Scalia once said that he was an originalist but he wasn't a nut, and he almost certainly had the paper-money issue in mind.

At the very least a judicial originalist faced with that sort of disaster would have some duty to figure out a way to manage the transition from the unconstitutional world of paper money to a constitutionally acceptable world with only metal coins. The most obvious way, I think, would be to delay the effective date of the

Court's judgment for long enough to allow Congress to propose and the states to ratify a constitutional amendment authorizing paper money. And, not incidentally, the example shows that being a nutty originalist might not be socially disastrous unless there are so many wrong decisions that nonetheless make good policy sense that devising glide paths to sensible results is simply too difficult.

That's not how most judicial originalists (and academic originalists who think they have something worthwhile to say about the matter) actually try to reconcile originalism and precedent.

1. *"Not a problem."* Wrong precedents are a problem for originalists only if they are wrong but socially beneficial. If the precedents are wrong and (in the originalists' eyes) bad policy, getting rid of the precedents makes us better off. There's a lurking rhetorical problem here for originalists: Their official theory tells them that judges shouldn't pay attention to the policy wisdom of competing interpretations of constitutional provisions. So they can't say openly that overruling a mistaken non-originalist precedent is no big deal because the precedent was bad for society.

Maybe there are some escape hatches. If the mistaken precedent *limits* government power, an originalist judge can say, "Maybe limiting government power in that way is a good idea; maybe it's a bad one. By overruling the precedent all I'm doing is letting today's voters and their representatives decide what policy they want." That's explicitly what Justice Alito wrote when the Court overruled *Roe v. Wade.*

Where the precedent *authorizes* the government to act—to regulate manufacturing, for example—that response isn't available: "Sure it might be good policy to let Congress regulate manufacturing but the Constitution doesn't allow it." Still, the judge can say, "If enough people think that letting Congress regulate manufacturing is a good idea they can amend the Constitution."

This is different, however, from the "well, go ahead and enact the policy you want" response to decisions overruling limits on government power. There today's voters can get what they want through ordinary majority-based legislation. The Constitution requires a super-majority to get a constitutional amendment.

The "no problem" position, then, might rest on an unstated and inescapably political view that it's better for government to do less than more.

2. *"Wrong the day it was decided."* You might think that to an originalist every decision that reached the wrong result about original public meaning was wrong the day it was decided. That phrase, though, is reserved for a handful of decisions that were *really really* wrong—*Dred Scott*, holding that people of African descent couldn't be citizens of the United States, *Plessy v. Ferguson*, upholding the constitutionality of statutes requiring racial segregation, *Korematsu v. United States*, upholding the creation of concentration camps for Japanese Americans during World War II, and, for today's Court, *Roe v. Wade*.

"Wrong the day it was decided" intensifies the wrongness of the decision's departure from originalism. What's the reason for the intensification? Almost certainly that the decision was also wrong along some other dimension—in the key cases, a dimension of moral or political theory: *Dred Scott, Plessy,* and *Korematsu* were wrong on that dimension because they endorsed morally repugnant racism.

The next step is to note some minor embarrassments about treating these cases as wrong along the originalist dimension. Chief Justice Roger Brooke Taney's decision in *Dred Scott* was explicitly originalist. Framing part of his discussion with reference to "the state of public opinion in relation to that unfortunate race, which prevailed . . . when the Constitution of the United States was framed and adopted," he wrote that the proposition that people of African descent "had no rights which the white man was bound to respect" was an "axiom in morals as well as in politics, which no one . . . supposed open to dispute."

There's no guarantee that originalism will be done well, of course, and this could be an example of bad originalism. Yet, there's pretty clearly something to Taney's claims about the original public meaning of the phrase "citizens of the United States." I don't know of a comprehensive originalist refutation of Taney's argument. There are scattered observations about the fact that descendants of Africans were treated as citizens in some Northern states in 1789, but that's an "original expected applications" point. And there's a lot of criticism from originalists about another part of Taney's opinion, which held that the Missouri Compromise violated the due process clause by preventing enslavers from taking their "property" into new states in the Midwest. I've called this a minor embarrassment because, in the end, originalists might produce a broader refutation.

Plessy and *Korematsu* raise a problem we've seen before. They are wrong on originalist grounds only if some constitutional provision was understood as barring the state and national governments from using racial categories. And here some earlier points recur. It's not clear that the Fourteenth Amendment's equal protection clause can do that work with respect to state governments, and it's pretty clear that the Fifth Amendment's due process clause can't do it with respect to the national government. Maybe the citizenship clauses can, although the originalist case to that effect hasn't been fully developed yet. And, in any event, it's almost certain that such a case will end up relying on the "concept/conception" distinction that plays a role in important non-originalist constitutional theory.

And that, at last, is the point of this excursion into originalism and precedent. When examined carefully, "wrong the day it was decided" points to the possibility that what judges actually do is pluralist. They use text and original public meaning and moral and political theory. You can call that a pluralist constitutional theory if you want. I think it's better to call it judging.

* * *

The next chapter develops the case for judging (and the case against constitutional theory) by examining the political and intellectual background of the rise of constitutional theory in the late twentieth century and the attempts by originalists to say that theirs is the only defensible constitutional theory, and specifically to say that pluralism and "reasoned judgment" can't possibly satisfy the requirements for an acceptable constitutional theory. That might be true given the disconnect between the practice of developing and defending constitutional theory and the practice of judging. But then as ordinary citizens (not as academics) we ought to ask ourselves, "Why care?"

CHAPTER 5

Why It Doesn't Take a Theory to Beat a Theory

The contrast I've drawn between theory and practice is all well and good but it scarcely shows up in today's discussions about the Constitution. Instead, there's a regular trope in those discussions, quoted by Ruth Marcus, for example: "It takes a theory to beat a theory." The idea is simple. You can point out all sorts of flaws in any particular constitutional theory, but unless you come up with a different one with fewer flaws, the only candidate for a theory is the imperfect one. And, the argument goes, imperfection is better than nothing, particularly in theory-land. As I argued in Chapter 4, for example, when critics identified problems with a specific version of originalism, originalists were able to come up with patches or reformulations or transformations that preserved the originalist impulse. The practice of academic theory, Stanley Fish might say, consists in large part of identifying and then fixing imperfections in the theories on offer.

Does it take a theory to beat a theory, though? Dean Erwin Chemerinsky's book is titled *Worse Than Nothing*. That's his description of originalism: Its flaws are so severe that giving it up would make us better off even if we don't immediately have at hand a better theory.

This chapter questions the proposition that you have to have some better theory in hand before you abandon a flawed one. I begin with a brisk overview of why theories that compete with originalism aren't better *as theories* than originalism, then offer a short intellectual history of the "takes a theory" aphorism in an effort to shed some light on why it took hold. The chapter then takes on the "takes a theory" proposition directly, arguing that sometimes even theorists should acknowledge that it doesn't always take a theory to beat a theory. It next returns to the perspective offered in this book, that practice can and does beat theory. It concludes by addressing Justice Antonin Scalia's assertion that practice in the form of reasoned or good judgment is an "outrageous" (his term) assertion of personal predilection and not a disciplined exercise that could be the institutional settlement that constitutional theory properly seeks.

A REALLY BRIEF LOOK AT NON-ORIGINALIST CONSTITUTIONAL THEORIES

What competition does originalism have in the race to the top of the theory hill? Here are the leading ones, with comments on the problems they face.

The moral reading of the Constitution. Closely associated with the legal philosopher Ronald Dworkin, this approach, when stripped of bells and whistles, basically tells courts that they should Do the Right Thing. Constitutional theory, though, begins with reasonable disagreement about what the Right Thing is. The moral reading would thus seem to be a non-starter. As I suspect many readers do, I experience arguments asserting that thus-and-so is what the moral reading of the Constitution is as attempts by an author with better rhetorical skills than I (but no greater moral insight) to pound me into submission. That's not surprising where disagreement is reasonable, as it often is: Moral readings say in essence that people who disagree are unreasonable.

In its most direct form the moral-reading approach doesn't even attempt to fit itself into the structure of constitutional theory's institutional settlement. Sometimes its supporters gesture toward doing so. They can't really say that courts are better than legislatures in coming up with the Right Thing; disagreement about what the Right Thing is means that we don't have good standards for figuring out what "better" might mean here.

They might claim that courts are better than legislatures in bringing out and openly assessing everything we should think about as we try to figure out what to do. It's not clear that this is true either. Court opinions rely on legal doctrines that sometimes obfuscate rather than reveal what should matter. The Supreme Court says that campaign finance regulations are content-based rules that can be justified only by a narrow list of "compelling" public interests. Put aside how the Court has applied that doctrine and think about what your mind is directed to by the doctrine ("are the regulations really based on content or on something else?," "what's a compelling interest?"), then think about how campaign finance regulation is discussed in Congress. Go through that exercise on other issues that the moral reading places at its heart, such as abortion. Jeremy Waldron actually looked at legislative discussions about abortion in the United Kingdom and found them substantially richer than the discourse in the U.S. Supreme Court.

I believe that Waldron's conclusion is broadly accurate, with one important exception. When legislators deal with proposals that would hurt despised minorities and deliberately so, what they say is often indefensible morally. One thing might be said in favor of legislators even here. Open racism and its cousins might be preferable to the genteel and subterranean racism that one finds in, for example, Chief Justice John Roberts's opinion upholding Donald Trump's so-called Muslim ban. Trump was open about his racism; seeing the racism in the chief justice's opinion takes some work. A constitutional system that ends up with a Muslim ban isn't good, but it's probably better if the ban's racism is fully open to view.

There is a connection, though, between this critique of the moral-reading approach and my overall argument for judging as a practice not determined by theory. Legal doctrine is a drawback for the moral-reading approach; it is at the heart of the judging-as-practice approach—it is, to quote Charles Fried again, what lawyers know.

Living constitutionalism (and common-law constitutionalism). The term "living constitutionalism" is batted around in part because originalism is a theory about what people long dead said, meant, or understood. Exactly what a living-Constitution interpretive approach is, however, isn't entirely clear. A first cut might be that the courts should interpret the Constitution to make it compatible with today's values.

The problem with that is almost as obvious as the problem with the moral-reading approach. Consider first what a "living Constitution" judge says in upholding a recently enacted statute: "This one is fine because it's consistent with today's values (even if it's inconsistent with what the Constitution's terms were understood to mean in 1789)." Next, what the same judge says in striking down such a statute: "This is unconstitutional because it's inconsistent with today's values."

We should immediately think, "Hold on a minute. Why are you better at figuring out what today's values are than representatives elected by the very people whose values you say you're enforcing?" Here are some answers.

(1) "This is an old, outdated statute; the people's values have changed since it was enacted." Fair enough if true—but inapplicable to recent statutes. And, if it's really inconsistent with today's values, why does it stay on the books and have legal force? The usual answer: because it's harder to repeal a statute than to enact one, particularly when other issues press for more urgent resolution. One implication of that observation might be, though, that the old statute really isn't all that inconsistent with today's values.

So maybe on this theory the courts can cleanse the statute books of old statutes that only a minority, though perhaps a decent-sized one (25 percent? one-third?), supports.

(2) "This statute does reflect the values of this particular legislature's constituents, but those constituents' values are out of line with the values of the American people as a whole." Maybe this will do for recently enacted statutes that are truly outliers in the nation as a whole. Still, one can have misgivings. The United States has a federal system, and one thing about federalism is that it allows communities to enforce their own values even when they differ from those of people elsewhere. And maybe a recently enacted statute really is an outlier but is ahead of the curve of changing national values: The legislature happened to see where the nation was moving and got where other legislatures will get in the future—if the courts don't stop them by invalidating the outlier-because-prescient statute.

(3) More promising: "You passed this in a hurry, after some scandal or outrageous incident, and you didn't really think hard about all of your own values that the statute is inconsistent with." Here too, maybe so, though we'd have to be careful not to let courts say that they know the legislature acted impulsively because they disagree with what it did. More important, this answer should allow the legislature—after a sober second thought, as it's sometimes put—to reenact the statute (without amending the constitution). Some nations have "override" provisions with that effect, but not the United States. Our institutional settlement rules out this answer to the objection to living constitutionalism.

(4) Also promising: "This statute doesn't actually reflect the values of the legislature's constituents because some of them were excluded from participating in ways that would build their values into the outcome and because some values were blocked from expression." As we saw in Chapter 2, this is John Hart Ely's constitutional theory—and if living constitutionalism ends up relying

on Ely-like ideas we probably should abandon living constitutionalism and take on Ely directly.

Ely's representation-reinforcing review. The idea is simple and intuitively appealing. We rely on our legislatures to represent all of us, and make laws that reflect our values. But if some of us don't have a chance to explain our values because some other law prevents us from making speeches or running advertisements telling other people (including candidates for office) what we believe, our representatives won't know what values the entire "we" have and won't develop statutes that accommodate everyone's views. Similarly if some of us can't vote at all. Legislators will worry about whether they're doing what the people who vote for them and might vote against them want. They won't worry about people who can't vote. And again the laws they enact won't reflect contemporary values taken as a whole. And sometimes legislators will adopt laws solely out of their own self-interest, not ours, just so that they can keep their seats.

The core problem with this approach is that it can do either too much or too little—which is to say, it's a vehicle for interpreters to do what they think the Right Thing is. Developing that argument in detail would take us too far afield, but I'll sketch the outlines of the problems.

Consider two interest groups, one focusing on criminal justice and the other on sexually explicit material on social media. The first group lobbies for increasing sentences for those who commit violent crimes, the other for a law restricting sexually explicit material. The first group supplies testimony from victims of violent crimes and their families, who describe the hurt they feel when offenders who harmed them are let out of prison too quickly, and the second group does the same with testimony from victims damaged by the distribution of sexually explicit "revenge porn" on social media. These groups aren't the only ones in the field, though. They are opposed by others, who supply testimony from the families of offenders who describe the harms to their families and communities that happen when so many people are removed from their families and surroundings for such a long time, and from people who explain how attempts to restrict material on social media inevitably overshoot and hit people who—to take a famous example—use a picture of a naked breast as part of a breast cancer awareness campaign.

At the end of all this lobbying, the legislature adopts both proposals by similar margins. The sentencing revision gets a free pass under this approach because it doesn't have anything to do with expression. The social-media law does deal with free expression and it gets examined carefully. Why, though, aren't the cases exactly the same? There were people for and against each proposal, each side fully aired its concerns, and one side won, the other lost. You can come up with fancy arguments about second-order concerns to try to patch this up but in the end it's going to be difficult to explain why the social-media law isn't just an ordinary example of how some people win and others lose in politics.

Justice Alito made this point, and connected it to the one I take up next, in a ham-handed way in *Dobbs*. Maybe, he wrote, women didn't have the right to vote when some restrictive abortion laws were adopted. Today, though, women have the right to vote and (he implied) there's no reason to think that their voices won't be heard in *today*'s legislatures—or, as it turned out, in referendums on protecting the right to reproductive choice. If enough women and their male allies have enough votes they can get restrictive laws repealed and replaced with permissive ones. The observation was ham-handed in part because it ignored the fact noted above that it's harder to get a legislature to repeal and replace a law than it is to get it to enact a new one (pure repeal is easy but its supporters will often divide on what to replace the old law with) and because it ignored the severe costs many women would incur between the day *Dobbs* was decided and the day a permissive law might come into effect. Still, it's worth reflecting on the possibility that Justice Alito's observation will make sense two or three election cycles down the road.

For voting exclusions we have to distinguish between formal exclusions from the vote and informal ones. Voter ID laws are formal exclusions: You show up to vote without an acceptable ID and you're turned away. Formal exclusions used to be common—Blacks weren't allowed to vote in the Jim Crow South, women weren't allowed to vote until the 1910s, and, it should be noted, children aren't allowed to vote today. And that last exclusion pinpoints the problem associated with formal exclusions. The ones we have today are supported by reasoned arguments—immaturity and domination by parents for children, avoiding fraud for voter IDs. We don't demand strong justifications for keeping kids from voting (some kids are far more mature than their parents, after all)—some decent reason will do.

But, you will already have thought, what about the fact that voter ID laws appear to prevent more Black than white people from voting, more poor people than richer ones? Now we're into the domain of informal "exclusions"—you have the right to vote but as a real-world matter you can't exercise it on equal terms with others. Informal exclusions matter for the same reason that formal ones do. Legislators won't care about the true impact of their actions because they won't worry about losing the votes of the informally excluded.

Here the problem is that we can proliferate informal exclusions pretty much at liberty. Critics of affirmative action, for example, argue that white "ethnics"—Americans of Polish or Italian ancestry—are informally excluded from decision-making in elite universities. The premise of the "Black Lives Matter" movement is that Blacks are informally excluded from all sorts of decision-making processes. Precisely because the exclusions are informal we can't rely on anything we can find in writing; we're driven to the theories of how American society actually works that lie in the background, and those background "sociological" or "political" theories will drive our conclusions—which is, again, exactly what constitutional theory tries to prevent.

Finally, what about laws that keep the "ins" in and protect them from defeat by the "outs"? Here the problem is the same as the one I just raised. Almost *everything* a sensible legislator does is aimed at making it easier for her to be reelected, harder for her to be defeated. Drawing district lines—gerrymandering—and campaign finance regulations that inevitably favor major party candidates are the most obvious examples. But think about why Democrats are happy to call the Affordable Care Act Obamacare: The statute turns out to be really popular, and branding it as a Democratic program gives a boost to Democratic candidates.

Deference and "minimalism." In a paper presented at the Chicago World's Fair in 1893, the Harvard Law professor James Bradley Thayer described "the American Doctrine of Constitutional Law," that courts should hold statutes unconstitutional only when the legislature (and the president signing them) "have not merely made a mistake, but have made a very clear one—so clear that it is not open to rational question." Today we can see Thayer's argument as an optimist's version of Ely's theory: Legislators generally did their best to do right by the Constitution, and (we would add today) there's no obvious reason to think that legislators are systematically worse than judges when each group tries its best.

Today, I think, we look at legislators with gimlet eyes and at judges with stars in our eyes. Even were we completely clear-eyed, though, there's reason to worry about Thayer's deferential approach to legislation. For starters it paints over the line dividing the Constitution as recommendation from the Constitution as binding law almost to the vanishing point. As binding law Thayer's Constitution rules out only laws that can be defended only by invoking truly crazy constitutional interpretations. Crazy interpretations do exist, today mostly among conspiratorial right-wing groups, as the law professor Jared Goldstein has admirably shown. He also shows, though, that crazy interpretations almost never have produced enacted laws.

There's another problem. Find a statute you think is clearly unconstitutional. Did the Supreme Court uphold it anyway? Were the justices in the majority crazy? If the Court struck it down, were there any dissenters (and were they crazy)? The testing case here is *Brown v. Board of Education,* a unanimous decision finding racial segregation of the public schools unconstitutional. Is there a non-crazy way of defending such segregation? Here's one possibility. A long tradition of Black nationalism defends the existence of separate Black institutions—most notably in this context elite segregated public high schools and historically Black colleges and universities—as important locations for the development and strengthening of a vibrant and self-sustaining Black community. Choosing to send your kids to such schools and to patronize Black businesses isn't crazy. And—here's the tricky part—having a strong Black community is a *social* benefit, not merely an individual one. That means that some parents won't choose to support separate institutions—and if enough of them opt out, the social benefits to the Black community dissipate. So government coercion in the form of segregation laws is required. I'm not endorsing this argument: just laying it out to present it as non-crazy even if wrong.

Cass Sunstein seemingly endorsed a modern version of Thayer's deference in advocating for what he called "minimalism" in deciding cases. As Sunstein put it, minimalism means deciding one case at a time, refraining from articulating broad or deep explanations for the case's outcome. John Roberts offered his version of minimalism: "If it is not necessary to decide more to a case, then in my view it is necessary not to decide more to a case." All the work here is being done by the word "necessary." Sunstein and

Roberts agree that sometimes the Court *should* issue broad and deep rulings; that's the burden of Roberts's decision in the affirmative action cases discussed in the next chapter. Not being a theorist, Roberts hasn't come up with an account of when minimalism should be foregone. Sunstein suggests that the degree of breadth and depth should be calibrated with preserving the Court's standing among the public in mind. This isn't a normative theory but a political one. And, I'd note, it's not at all clear that the people we pick as judges are much good at gauging what will build and what will undermine public support. For several decades, for example, conservatives on the Court thought that *Roe v. Wade* was undermining public support for the Court. When they overruled *Roe* they discovered they were wrong: the *Dobbs* decision did more to undermine the Court's position among the public than almost any other recent decision.

Of course there's much more to be said about these approaches to constitutional theory, but this should be enough to show that each has problems at least as serious as those associated with originalism. And, as with originalism, you can patch things up with increasingly complex distinctions—and thereby weaken the ability of the theory to do theory's job of steering judges away from simply Doing the Right Thing.

And of course there are other candidates, because success in the legal academy depends in part upon a scholar's ability to come up with something new. In my view most, probably all, of the other candidates offer variants of or tweaks to the three major ones. The problems I've identified suggest why originalists don't think the alternatives are good enough to beat originalism as a constitutional theory.

One final point before taking on the "takes a theory" aphorism directly. As Stanley Fish suggested, sometimes theory is among the resources good lawyers and judges use as they engage in law-as-practice. Good lawyers and judges undoubtedly can and do pick up bits and pieces of the moral reading, living constitutionalism, and representation-reinforcing review as they construct their arguments. That too is what we saw in Chapter 2. When they do so, though, they are practicing law, not applying constitutional theory.

WHERE "IT TAKES A THEORY" CAME FROM

Now to the aphorism. Marcus quotes the "takes a theory" aphorism from the law professor Richard Epstein, who describes himself as a classical liberal. Epstein offers a rather libertarian anti-government form of classical liberalism that finds support in the market-oriented economic theories developed initially in the late nineteenth century and then elaborated with a great deal of supporting mathematical apparatus by Chicago-school economists in the twentieth century. Richard Posner drew upon the same material to create the field of law-and-economics. The connection between the aphorism and economics (and law-and-economics) is brought out by a more detailed account of the aphorism in the extremely valuable "Legal Theory Lexicon" written by Lawrence Solum. Solum traces the aphorism's appearance to Epstein and supports his exposition of its meaning with a quotation from the economist George Stigler (a colleague of Epstein's at the University of Chicago), and a reference to the law-and-economics scholar Thomas Ulen.[1]

The connection between the "takes a theory" aphorism and law-and-economics arises, I believe, from the deep aspiration of constitutional theory to overcome disagreements about the Right and the Good through an institutional settlement that narrows—and perhaps eliminates—the range of reasonable disagreement. Here's how the argument goes. Science gives us all the firmest

1. Solum's attribution to Epstein accords with my recollection of the way the aphorism entered the discourse of constitutional theory.

possible foundation for agreement because it identifies features of the real world that each of us can investigate and confirm for ourselves. At least in part for that reason lawyers everywhere have been attracted to the idea that law was or could become a science. The closest thing we have to a true social science is economics. (Note that I'm describing the argument here, not endorsing it.) After all, there's a Nobel Prize for economic *science*.[2] And how does theory-change occur in economics and physics? When someone comes up with a better theory, one that beats the prevailing wisdom. So, if law's search for something that leads to reducing disagreement is like science's search for objectivity, theory-change in law should have the same form: It Takes a Theory to Beat a Theory in physics, economics, and law.

This is a neat story but it runs up against two related difficulties. (1) We have a traditional story about how one theory in physics (and maybe economics) beats another but it's not clear how we can tell that story about law. (2) And the traditional story might not be accurate even for physics (and probably isn't for economics). We have to go on an excursion into the philosophy and history of science before we get the payoff for law.

The traditional story about theory change. Scientists glean facts from experiments and other observations about the world. They construct theories that account for—explain—these facts. The theories suggest other experiments and possible observations that might bolster—or, importantly, undermine—the theories. When these new observations don't quite fit the prevailing theory, scientists tinker with the theory. Sometimes, though, the anomalies accumulate to the point where the theoretical structure looks unwieldy or too complicated. Some scientists come up with another

2. Technically, and I think not without significance, it's the National Bank of Sweden Prize for Economic Science in Memory of Alfred Nobel and was created in 1968, well after the original prizes were first awarded.

theory that accounts for all the observed facts more elegantly and suggests new experiments and observations. After some time passes the new theory beats the old one because it does a better job of accounting for all the observable facts and has succeeded in generating experiments that "confirm" the theory by producing previously unknown facts that fit the theory.

It should be pretty clear how hard it should be to tell *that* story about how one constitutional theory might beat another. For starters (and maybe finishers), what are the facts for which the competing theories offer explanations? Decisions (in the past?) by the Supreme Court? I argued in Chapter 2 that when you look at those decisions you just won't find a single theory at work. Even worse, what are the as-yet-unknown facts that "experiments" might reveal? Next year's Supreme Court decisions? Any working majority on the Court can defeat any theory by disregarding it.

Maybe theories compete over which one provides a more stable institutional settlement—reduces disagreement more than the other candidates about what doing the Right Thing means for courts and legislatures. One theory is better when it's simpler and more consistent. As we've seen, though, all the candidate theories are really terrible along those dimensions. When worked out to be intellectually defensible they're all really complicated and judges never apply them consistently (again, maybe the case is different for academic theories). And I don't think we have a "metric" to measure which one is less bad than another. How would you go about elaborating the "worse" part of this sentence: "Sure, originalism isn't very good at achieving simplicity and consistency but living constitutionalism is worse"?

This might suggest—it does suggest to me—that the scientific model that generates the "It Takes a Theory" aphorism is simply inapposite to law. More directly, law might not be a science at all, in which case we can't use the scientific model to come up with criteria for figuring out when one theory is better than another.

You might want to consider here what happens in philosophy, another discipline concerned about the Right and the Good. Philosophy has many more competing theories than today's constitutional theory world. Outside a world of academic politics and a certain kind of personal polemics, philosophers don't think that their job is to decide whether Kant beats Mill or, to use an example from John Hart Ely, Rawls beats Nozick. Some philosophers do think that Kant has better arguments than Mill and try to explain why. They know, though, that these discussions have gone on for centuries and are going to continue: Kant is *never* going to beat Mill in any interesting sense. Rather, the best philosophers see their job as engaging in a conversation about the Right and the Good that will help people better understand the decisions they have to make.

Though philosophy might provide an alternative model for "theory" than science, it's different from law, at least from the law that judges have to make or apply. Philosophers can engage in endless conversation that educates them and us about our choices. Judges have to make decisions. Perhaps the model of conversation might caution a judge against having too much confidence that her decision is right even though she has to stick with it. Now, though, we're well outside the domain of constitutional theory— and perhaps that's a good thing because law just isn't a science and doesn't need theories (or stories about theory-change) that take science as their model.

A revised story about theory change in science. In 1962 the physicist and historian of science Thomas Kuhn transformed the study of theory-change in science. He accepted the story about accumulating anomalies but gave it a different spin. Scientific theories can deal with essentially every anomaly by making adjustments within the theory that preserve its coherence, though at the expense of simplicity. Someone who finds the complexity intellectually unsatisfying comes up with a competing "paradigm." Adherents of the prevailing theory point out correctly that the new paradigm actually does a worse job explaining all the facts than their own. Proponents of the new theory ignore them, hoping that further development of their theory will eventually deal with the things it doesn't handle well initially. They generate new experiments and observations that wouldn't be suggested by the prevailing theory and—when the observations fit the new theory but not the old one—continue to work on the new theory.

This approach has lots of interesting illustrations. One of my favorites is a thought expressed by Norwood Hanson, another historian and philosopher of science: Of some novel observation, Hanson said in effect, "You couldn't see it until you believed it." That is, accepting a theory was a requirement of seeing some fact about the world—the reverse of the traditional thought that theories are constructed from observed facts about the world. Related: Proponents of the new theory look for facts that are consistent with their theory but not with the prevailing one. Experiments are always messy, though, and you have to interpret the results. You discard some because you found out that something had contaminated the apparatus, for example. And more interesting, you resolve ambiguities in the observations systematically to favor your new theory.

Theory-change in science turns out to be messier than the traditional story has it. The bottom line is that one theory beats another only in part because it's better at accounting for the facts. Two other reasons are age—the adherents of the older theory simply die off—and institutional prestige, as proponents of the new theory are either sponsored by or come to take positions in high-prestige institutions.

And that, finally, is the payoff for constitutional theory. Simplicity and consistency have something to do with theory-change but not all that much because every theory is complicated and applied inconsistently. Demographics matter: How is support for one or another theory distributed by age? What theories do younger versus older judges and scholars accept? And so does prestige: For academic theories, are the proponents professors at top five or top ten law schools? And, probably most important, what theories do Supreme Court justices say they follow?

The causal chain doesn't run like this: The Supreme Court's justices have come to accept originalism because it's the best constitutional theory. The causal chain runs the other way: Originalism is today's best theory because the Supreme Court's justices have come to accept it. And the well-established story about originalism's connection to the conservative challenge to the Warren Court explains why.

THREE WAYS OF TRYING TO FIND OUT
WHEN ONE THEORY BEATS ANOTHER

Suppose we did want to put theories in competition. How could we tell that one beat another?

Like scientists, we might *experiment*. We could use one theory for a while, then switch to another for a while, then assess the human condition at the end of each period. Maybe that's how we should understand what's going on in the United States today: an experiment in originalist constitutional theory. The difference between this and what happens in science is obvious: We have no mechanism to stop the experiment if we think it's not working out.[3]

We can *compare* systems. See how systems in which one theory prevails do as compared with systems in which another theory prevails. All such comparative exercises run up against serious problems of method. Not only might it be difficult to find places where we can confidently say, "Yup, they're using that theory," but

---

3. There's an important literature in the history of science devoted precisely to the question, When do scientists decide to end an experiment?

conditions across the systems are going to be so different that we can't possibly be confident that we should attribute any differences we observe, particularly with respect to something as general as "human well-being," to their different constitutional theories.

For a while we might have looked at Canada, whose judges said for a while that their constitution was a "living tree," perhaps akin to living constitutionalism in the United States. Even if we put to one side all the jokes about how Canada is really different from the United States, there's a problem of timing. Until recently the U.S. Supreme Court didn't adhere to a single constitutional theory, so we'd probably have to compare the United States today with Canada a generation or two ago when living-tree constitutionalism flourished. Changes in historical conditions are as confounding as changes in geography. And, if we tried to compare the United States and Canada today we'd run across the difficulty that living-tree constitutionalism in Canada has been weakened by an infusion of something akin to originalism.

Another possibility is to compare *state* supreme courts in the United States. Some are originalist, some are living-constitutionalist. How do they compare in terms of well-being? Diversity among the states isn't as deep as diversity across nations but it's enough to make that comparison difficult—as is the pervasive influence of the U.S. Supreme Court on the way judges everywhere in the United States think about constitutions.

Finally, there's the possibility of *history*: compare then and now in the United States. The problems I've already described recur here. And, I should emphasize, Chapter 2, which did look back to the 1930s, wasn't designed as an exercise in comparing then and now; I used the 1930s to illustrate what it looks like when judges decide cases without using constitutional theory.

In the end, then, I'm inclined to think that we couldn't figure out whether one theory beat another even if we tried—another reason for thinking that the "takes a theory" aphorism has something wrong built into it.

TWO REASONS WHY SOMETIMES IT DOESN'T TAKE A THEORY TO BEAT A THEORY

The examination of originalism in Chapter 4 showed one reason for rejecting a proposed theory without having a substitute available. The first originalists proposed what they called a jurisprudence of original intentions. Where "intentions" was understood to mean "what the relevant actors had in their minds," a jurisprudence of original intentions was subject to objections that even its proponents came to accept. The jurisprudence of original intentions failed because it didn't make intellectual sense.

That didn't mean that originalism disappeared. It was underdeveloped and then it got better. A first stab, with original expected applications, helped but also met objections that originalism's proponents thought cogent. So they modified the theory again, to original public meaning (where original expected applications were relevant but not conclusive).

Now consider the "takes a theory" aphorism in light of the second "Kuhnian" version of theory change. Somebody puts up "living constitutionalism" or something else as an alternative to fully developed originalism. Originalists point out flaws in the proposal and say, "You don't have a theory that beats ours." It's clearly open to proponents of the alternative to say, "The flaws are indeed there, but that's simply because our theory is underdeveloped just as yours was. Give us a chance and we'll make it better." Supporters of the alternative agree that their current version doesn't beat fully developed originalism but think correctly that that's no reason to give up on it.

Here's a second reason for rejecting a theory without having a better one in hand. A constitutional theory can collapse of its own weight. Scientists like elegant theories, but if the world's so complicated that the only theory that explains it is complicated, so be it. The case of constitutional theory is different. To do its job a constitutional theory has to be reasonably simple so that the unsophisticated bozos get where the Supreme Court majority wants them to be. The more you have to patch it up the more a theory looks like a Rube Goldberg cartoon machine: Sure, if you put the ball in the top corner eventually it's going to tip over the milk carton to get the milk into a glass the waiting child can drink. The machine gets *that* job done just as a complicated theory generates results but it doesn't do so at all simply.

I argued in Chapter 4 that an intellectually defensible originalism—academic originalism—had become just that sort of Rube Goldberg machine, and that judicial originalism, a simpler version, wasn't and more important couldn't be applied consistently. Judicial originalism, then, can't do theory's job—and can be rejected even if you don't have a simple, well-developed alternative in hand that you think can be applied consistently.

Now comes the sting of this chapter's discussion of alternative theories. In intellectually defensible versions they're *all* too complicated. Constitutional theory as it is currently understood can't do what it's supposed to do.

PRACTICE AS THE ALTERNATIVE TO THEORY

By now it should be clear that I believe that practice is the alternative to theory. Of course judges who purport to follow their preferred theory think they're engaged in practice too. Maybe it's a mistake to use "practice" as a shorthand for "good judgment" and "reasoned judgment," but I think the term helpfully links my argument to Fried's and Fish's.

In Chapter 2, I argued that the Hughes Court's decisions brought out several characteristics of good judging. One was transparency, another that decisions have to be primarily legal in character. With more of the argument in hand we can reexamine those characteristics. Sometimes I think of complicated cases as something like a Grand Slalom: A judge starts at the top of the slope and has to navigate through a number of gates before reaching the finish line—the result she seeks. In the Jones & Laughlin case, for example, Chief Justice Hughes had to deal with the "flow of commerce" argument as it had developed in prior cases, the proposition that manufacturing was not commerce, and the "direct effects" doctrine. He maneuvered his way through them until he reached the Bituminous Coal Act case and he couldn't figure out what to do. So he simply slammed through the gate by saying that the case wasn't controlling.

Up to that point Hughes had offered entirely legal arguments. How then did he get to his result when he couldn't come up with a legal argument against the Coal Act decision? The answer is that he relied on something else—there (and in my view in most cases when legal reasons run out) a judgment about what good policy would be. Constitutional theory, or at least snippets of constitutional theory, might well have its place precisely here—not as driving the core analysis but as closing the gap between that analysis and the result the Court reaches.

What remains is a more detailed examination of the source of Justice Scalia's "outrage" (remember, his term) at the prospect that judges would exercise reasoned judgment. His reason, recall, was that he thought "reasoned judgment" was a mealy-mouthed way of saying "our personal predilections." "Reasoned judgment," for Justice Scalia, seems to be a version of the moral reading of the Constitution.

And indeed you can pick out—and Justice Scalia did—parts of the opinion he was attacking that sound in a sort of moral reading. The most prominent is what's become notorious among conservatives as the "sweet mystery of life" passage conventionally attributed to Justice Anthony Kennedy: "At the heart of liberty is the right to define one's own concept of existence, of meaning, of the universe, and of the mystery of human life." That does look like something you'd find in a treatise on moral philosophy.

Picking out an isolated passage, though, is a mistake when you're trying to figure out what "reasoned judgment" is. We've already seen that actual judicial practice involves taking a little bit of this, a little bit of that, and other bits and pieces and assembling them into an opinion. Recall that Justice Alito threw a little "representation-reinforcing review" into his originalist-dominated opinion in *Dobbs* and that the best explanation for the originalist position on decisions that were wrong the day they were decided is that an infusion of moral philosophy is sometimes appropriate.

A bit more on pluralism as a constitutional theory before concluding. Legal scholars who have looked at what the Court actually does know that the Court is eclectic or pluralist, as I've just described. Philip Bobbitt, for example, in a work that has had an enormous influence among legal scholars of constitutional law, identified a handful of what he called "modalities" of legal argument that could be found in the Court's opinions. Richard Fallon similarly identifies a number of interpretive techniques that the Court deploys.

My practice-based story about constitutional interpretation is in the same ballpark as theirs, with a twist. Fallon's analysis of the Court's recent decisions leads him to develop a hierarchy in the use of the interpretive techniques: originalism first, then moral principle, for example. Driving his analysis, though, is a concern for what he calls "implementation," the development of rules that officials, including lower court judges, can reliably follow to produce the best set of policies we can have. He argues that "independent judicial judgment" provides the first foundation for good implementation. My account tries to flesh out what independent judicial judgment entails.

Bobbitt's presentation is more idiosyncratic. After developing his account of "modalities," he turned to explaining why giving judges a choice among modalities was a good thing. Doing so, he argued, allowed them to take moral responsibility for what they were doing. Despite its somewhat peculiar phrasing, that seems to me right. I'd put it a bit differently, though: It allows them to be lawyers.

CONCLUSION

I inserted the word "our" into Justice Scalia's reference to personal predilections only in part because he was quoting from an opinion published as the joint work of three of his colleagues. The more important reason for the insertion is to emphasize that what he was describing wasn't merely the personal musings of an individual (like Ronald Dworkin) who's trying to get us to agree with his personal views. They were the product of discussion and deliberation among a group of people—there, only three, but for "reasoned judgment" more broadly, discussion and deliberation within the much larger community of lawyers. That community determines through its practices of reward and commendation what counts as good or reasoned judgment. That's what the survey identifying great judges in Chapter 1 actually tells us: Who does the community regard as doing the job of judging particularly well?

I've already mentioned one implication of this way of thinking about law and judging as a practical not a theoretical activity. The implication is that "reasoned judgment" has a non-trivial sociological character. As the community of lawyers changes, what counts as good or reasoned judgment will change as well. Sometimes that change appears on the surface of opinions. I mentioned that today we wouldn't regard Chief Justice Hughes as having a good writing style because the community of lawyers has come to look for sentences and paragraphs that flow more freely than

Hughes's—and that are more conversational in non-technical cases. Sometimes the changes in the community of lawyers appear in demographics. A community of lawyers with 40 percent women (the figure for 2022) will have different standards of good judgment than a community with about 2.5 percent (the figure for 1940).

Before examining the implications of this sociological view of good judgment, Chapter 6 offers a detailed study of the Court's recent decision dealing with affirmative action in higher education, using theory and reasoned judgment as metrics.

CHAPTER 6

Students for Fair Admissions and the Craft of Judging

Maybe it doesn't take a theory to beat a theory, but we have to have ways of talking about what the Court does that don't simply reproduce the disagreements that going to court is supposed to resolve. And, as I've suggested, maybe my focus on judicial craft introduces a theory of sorts. Can it beat the more cosmic versions of constitutional theory?

This chapter tries to show that it can, through a reasonably close examination of the Supreme Court's decision in 2023 to invalidate race-based affirmative action admissions programs at elite universities. It isn't a law review article going into enormous detail about the ins and outs of every argument the justices made. Instead I ask whether their opinions are theory-driven or pluralist, and if the latter how good they are as a matter of judicial craft. My primary "case studies" are the opinion for the Court by Chief Justice Roberts and Justice Jackson's dissenting opinion, with a few glances at Justice Thomas and Justice Sotomayor's opinions.

I focus on four aspects of the opinions. (1) How do they use history? What versions of originalism, if any, do they use? Here my treatment engages rather directly theory as performed by judges. (2) How well do the opinions rely upon or distinguish the precedents about racial equality and affirmative action? (3) Do they come up with a workable doctrine to guide elite universities in developing admissions policies and lower courts in evaluating the constitutionality of those policies? (4) What tone do they adopt in dealing with arguments against their positions, especially those made by their colleagues, and in attempting to reach a wider audience in the informed general public?

My bottom-line judgment is this: Only Justice Thomas's opinion is particularly theory-driven and the other opinions are decent examples of good judicial craft. My personal view is that Justice Jackson's opinion does better along most of the dimensions of interest: It handles the history a bit better because it moves away from the rather general historical account the chief justice offers without getting bogged down in the kinds of details that bedevil Justice Thomas's opinion. Justice Jackson's opinion handles the precedents a bit better than the chief justice's, although here the chief justice was at a disadvantage because he was trying to work a substantial change while reconciling the new rule as best he could with the precedents. A closer question for me is tone: I think her tone toward both her colleagues and the general audience is a bit better than the chief justice's (and clearly better than Justice Sotomayor's as to her colleagues). And, of course, Justice Jackson didn't have to worry about creating a new and workable doctrine in the way the chief justice did.

Having said all this, I of course have to acknowledge that my relative ranking might well be affected by the fact that I agree with the outcome Justice Jackson reached, and I wouldn't fault anyone who reversed the rankings unless they treated Justice Jackson's opinion as plainly inadequate as a matter of judicial craft. And, perhaps more important, both opinions are decent enough but neither is, in my view, a great example of the judicial craft. That shouldn't come as a surprise. It would be a miracle if a justice happened to produce a great opinion just in time for me to use it in this book.

These observations lead to a more general point. Judgments about judicial craft are *collective*. They reflect what the legal profession as a whole takes to be the requirements of good judging. They inevitably consist of putting together what individual lawyers think about particular judges and cases, which is why what I personally think about the opinions in *SFFA* is relevant, but it's also why I don't take my personal evaluation as conclusive. These judgments are historically contingent as well. What counted as good judicial craft in the 1950s might not receive the same evaluation today. My personal standards were shaped in the late twentieth century and might not be the ones the profession adheres to now. And, worryingly, the polarization that we see in our politics—and in the Court's performance—may also fracture the bar to the point where we don't have generally agreed-upon criteria for determining what a good opinion is, or who a good judge is.

Still, I believe that attempting to look at opinions in light of craft-based criteria is worthwhile even with all those qualifications.

PRELIMINARIES

Here's a simplified account of how the admissions programs in *Students for Fair Admissions v. Harvard (SFFA)* and a parallel case against the University of North Carolina operated. Admissions officers read every applicant's file. The files included high school grades, the results of standardized tests, descriptions of the applicants' extracurricular activities, and whatever personal statements the applicants submitted. They then came to a "holistic" judgment about where the applicant ranked in the entire pool and made a recommendation about admission. In reaching that judgment they expressly gave special weight to race—that is, whether the applicant was African American. These recommendations moved on to committees with more members, who made the same kind of holistic judgment, ultimately resulting in decisions to admit or deny admission.

This process developed in response to the Supreme Court's decisions about the constitutionality of affirmative action programs. Again to oversimplify: *Regents of the University of California v. Bakke* (1978) held unlawful, by a five-to-four vote, a program at one of the university's medical schools that reserved 16 percent of an entering class's seats for racial minorities. Such quotas were impermissible. But, in what the Court came to treat as the controlling opinion, Justice Lewis F. Powell, Jr., wrote that elite universities could take race into account in an effort to put together a racially diverse class.

Grutter v. Bollinger (2003) upheld the admissions process at the University of Michigan's law school. A companion case involved Michigan's undergraduate school. That school assigned a fixed number to various items in applicants' files such as test scores and high school grades. It did the same for race. The Court held that this was too much like a quota and ruled it unconstitutional. The law school's process was different. Admissions officers took race into account in coming to an overall judgment ("holistic," as it came to be called) about where each applicant was in the admissions ranking. That, in Justice O'Connor's opinion for a divided Court, was constitutionally permissible.

Finally, *Fisher v. Texas* (2016) allowed Texas to take race explicitly into account in trying to put together classes that had a "critical mass"—in colloquial terms, "enough"—members of racial minorities.

What did the Court have to say about the Harvard and UNC programs and how they fared under these precedents?

THE USES OF HISTORY

After an eight-page introduction, Chief Justice Roberts offered an extremely brief (five-page) view from 30,000 feet of the history of the Constitution's equal protection clause and its interpretation from 1868 through the 1950s. This is his gesture toward originalism—a quite watered-down version. The opinion has a single paragraph on the discussion of the clause's meaning when it was adopted, quoting no more than a sentence from each of four of the clause's supporters. There's no explicit discussion of what ordinary people of the time understood the clause to mean.

The first sentence following the paragraph quoting the amendment's supporters is, "At first, this Court embraced the transcendent aims of the Equal Protection Clause." But, the chief justice continued, the Court and "the country [] quickly failed to live up to the Clause's core commitments." *Brown v. Board of Education,* invalidating racial segregation of public schools, recognized "the inevitable truth of the Fourteenth Amendment." That truth: The Constitution bars all laws expressly using racial classifications unless they "survive a daunting two-step examination known . . . as 'strict scrutiny,'" which requires that the classification "is used to 'further compelling governmental interests'" and is "narrowly tailored," meaning "'necessary[,] to achieve that interest.'" With rare exceptions, the Court had allowed express racial classifications to be used only in "remediating specific, identified instances of past [unlawful] discrimination."

You can read the chief justice's discussion here in a couple of ways, each of which poses some difficulties. A mildly originalist reading is that ordinary people in 1868 understood the equal protection clause to enact its "core commitments," but that that understanding was lost for a while until the Court retrieved it in *Brown.*[1] The difficulty here is that four quotations can't establish what ordinary people understood in 1868. You can bolster the

---

1. Political scientist and law professor Mark Graber observes that this reading is like "declar[ing] that the Oakland Athletics are the best team in baseball"

argument by saying that over time the American people came to understand the clause's true meaning, but that moves dangerously close (from a theory point of view) to living constitutionalism.

The simpler reading is that the equal protection clause enacted a "transcendent" meaning of equality—what equality really requires. Recall the version of originalism holding that the Constitution's general terms enact "concepts" rather than "conceptions." This too moves dangerously close to something the Court's conservatives generally oppose, a "moral reading" of the Constitution, a theory typically treated as an alternative to originalism. And, more important, this reading requires some defense of the proposition that equality really requires the Court's rule that express racial classifications are unconstitutional unless they survive strict scrutiny. The chief justice offers no such defense—or at least no explicit one. Perhaps he thought that the Court's rule was common sense or self-evident.

Perhaps, too, that thought is correct. Yet there's an obvious alternative concept available that accounts for all the material the chief justice presented. The alternative is that racial equality requires the Court's rule with respect to uses of race that *disadvantage racial minorities.* Here one of the basic lessons real historians teach—and a lesson that most people, including judges, have learned—is that we can understand what people say only by understanding the context in which they speak. The "transcendent" principle the chief justice identified was *always* set in the context of express racial classifications that disadvantaged African Americans and of course was entirely appropriate for that context. The chief justice's opinion quotes *Loving v. Virginia,* which held unconstitutional a state ban on interracial marriage, because the

by "point[ing] to the twenty games they have won while treating their sixty losses as exceptional."

Fourteenth Amendment "proscri[bes] . . . all invidious racial discrimination." He doesn't say anything, though, about what law professor Michael Dorf calls the "pesky" word *invidious*.[2] What people say in one context, though, doesn't necessarily carry over into other contexts. It might, but it requires argument to explain why it does. The chief justice didn't offer any such argument.

We can find an originalist strand in the chief justice's presentation: The equal protection clause's enactors understood that they were writing the concept of equality—what equality really means—into the Constitution, and our understanding of what equality means gradually unfolded as the nation and the Court confronted cases using express racial classifications. The weakness here isn't in theory—this is an available version of originalism—but in presentation. Making the argument requires a fair amount of fleshing out that the chief justice didn't provide, most notably in connection with the possibility that his transcendent principle applied only to disadvantaging uses of racial classifications.

If the chief justice's opinion looked at history from 30,000 feet, Justice Thomas's opinion looked at it on ground level. Adopting a more standard version of originalism, Justice Thomas "offer[ed] an originalist defense of the colorblind Constitution," devoting more than fifteen pages (not five) to examining what people said and did in 1868 and shortly thereafter to figure out what they understood the equal protection clause to mean.

Justice Thomas faced two main problems. He acknowledged that not "all of the individuals who put forth and ratified the Fourteenth Amendment" supported the colorblind Constitution idea, but "substantial evidence suggests" that the Fourteenth Amendment enacted that idea. He mustered an excerpt from the government's brief in *Brown* that asserted that "there were widespread

2. Dorf compiles other examples of quotations that ignore the context in which statements condemning racial classifications were made.

expressions of a general understanding of the broad scope of the Amendment." Especially because Justice Thomas also acknowledged that "the historical record . . . is sparse," this raises the 60–40 (or 70–30 problem) I discussed in Chapter 4.

The other problem he had to confront was that there were what he called "a smattering of federal and state statutes" that supporters of affirmative action said showed that the equal protection clause allowed governments to use racial classifications that *advantaged* racial minorities—a principle Justice Thomas disparaged as an "increasingly in vogue" "antisubordination" interpretation of the clause. As to the "in vogue," it's worth noting that when Justice Harlan introduced the phrase, "Our Constitution is color-blind," he preceded it with the sentence, "There is no caste here," which certainly can be given an "antisubordination" spin. Justice Thomas's rhetoric is notable: the "smattering" included the Freedmen's Bureau Acts, which were key features of congressional Reconstruction; the antisubordination interpretation is "increasingly in vogue"; and, reminding us that some originalists deal with the 60–40 problem by denying that the historical evidence is closely balanced, that interpretation "lacks any basis in the original meaning of the Fourteenth Amendment."

The work Justice Thomas did to deal with statutes like the Freedmen's Bureau Acts shows that "lacks any basis" is a substantial overstatement. Some were "formally race-neutral": They provided benefits to freedmen, not to all African Americans (though of course all freedmen were African Americans). It's hard to know what to make of this. I would have thought that a statute that provided benefits only to African Americans by describing their former status *was* a race-based classification—a racial gerrymander, if you will, that managed to target only African Americans without using racial terms.

Other statutes provided benefits to members of a class—African Americans, including those liberated from enslavement by the

North's victory in the Civil War and those who had been free persons of color before that—that had been systematically and, importantly, universally discriminated against. Justice Thomas treated these statutes as illustrations of the "remediation" interpretation the chief justice offered—or at least they were "likely" permissible for that reason. Some of Justice Thomas's formulations reveal the work he had to do: In putting aside a federal statute providing funds for "destitute colored people," Justice Thomas relied on a law review article by an originalist scholar, writing, "Congress thus *may have* enacted the statute not because of race, but rather to address a special problem in shantytowns . . . where blacks lived." Two points: "Likely" and "may have" again raise the 60–40 problem ("may have" implies "might not have"), and the point of strict scrutiny is to avoid direct inquiries into why legislatures enacted the statutes in question.

There are a few details to work out. The "remediation" interpretation, recall, requires that the prior discrimination was unlawful, not merely immoral, but the discrimination in the pre-war South was completely lawful at the time. The remedies might not be particularly well-tailored, because someone might receive an employment benefit as a remedy for discrimination in education (for Justice Thomas, narrow tailoring required that "attempts to remedy" past discrimination "must be closely tailored to address *that* particular" discrimination). And, the entire class benefited because of a legislative and social judgment that discrimination had been pervasive even though no African American established in any formal way that he or she had been discriminated against (was, in Justice Thomas's terms, an "identified victim[] of discrimination"). Think here of an African American child born in 1865 after enslavement ended who received an educational benefit from the Freedman's Bureau. These details might be taken to show that, as understood in the immediate aftermath of the Civil War, ordinary people understood that race-based "remedies" could be given if a legislature decided that society had been pervaded by wrongful though perhaps not unlawful discrimination. And that, affirmative action's supporters said, was precisely the case today—or at least democratically authorized decision-makers could so conclude.

Justice Thomas countered some of these arguments by pointing out that affirmative action's supporters didn't rely on the large number of statutes enacted after 1868 that expressly discriminated against African Americans, suggesting that this barred them from relying on a handful of statutes that provided benefits expressly to African Americans. That, though, simply reproduces the chief justice's mistake: What people said and did in connection with statutes imposing disadvantages on African Americans doesn't tell us what they understood the equal protection clause to mean when statutes purported to provide benefits on the basis of race.

None of this is to say that Justice Thomas's originalist case for the colorblind Constitution is indefensible. It's rather that, as we saw with the chief justice's use of history, Justice Thomas's opinion has gaps that need to be filled in for the defense to succeed fully. Those gaps are a signal of weaknesses in crafting the opinion.

Not committed to originalism as theory and not embarrassed about saying things about what equality really means, Justice Jackson dealt with history differently. She gave readers a history of race's impact on U.S. economic and social development, with the goal of establishing that differences in the social capital available today to whites and Blacks were the legacy of racial discrimination starting with slavery and continuing with government support through the twentieth century. This isn't anything like originalism, though Justice Jackson touched upon the short period surrounding Reconstruction when national policy, including the Fourteenth Amendment, seemed set on transforming the society. That transformation, for Justice Jackson, at least permitted—she emphasized that it didn't require—democratically responsible bodies to adopt programs that offset the accumulated race-related differences in social capital.

Qua history, her essay was reasonably powerful. The difficulty is that the Court's precedents appeared to say that that history was *doctrinally* irrelevant to the question of affirmative action's constitutionality.

HANDLING THE PRECEDENTS

Justice Jackson's historical narrative strongly suggested that affirmative action *should* be justified on justice-related grounds: distributive justice, meaning that social goods should be shared by all significant groups in proportion to their presence in the overall population unless there's some strong alternative to racism as an explanation for group-related disparities; restorative justice, meaning that affirmative action was justified as a way of placing African Americans in positions they would have occupied had race discrimination disappeared after the Civil War; or compensatory justice, meaning that affirmative action was a way of paying African Americans back for the harms done in the course of the history Justice Jackson recounted.

It's probably worth noting that for many of affirmative action's supporters, these justice-related justifications are what really motivated their support. To take one example: President Lyndon Johnson's famous commencement speech at Howard University, said, "You do not take a person who, for years, has been hobbled by chains and liberate him, bring him up to the starting line of a race and then say, 'you are free to compete with all the others,' and still justly believe that you have been completely fair." This pretty clearly alludes to a restorative justice argument.

Justice Jackson's doctrinal problem was that *Bakke* had expressly said that none of these justice-related reasons could justify affirmative action; only diversity could. Not surprisingly, elite universities climbed on board the diversity train—and, I emphasize, their leaders sincerely came to believe that diversity was indeed an important educational value. But, with the justice-related arguments ruled out, Justice Jackson was forced into explaining why UNC's affirmative action program did indeed satisfy strict scrutiny. She tried, but the analytical structure she had erected was completely disconnected from diversity. For all practical purposes, *any* diversity-related program would do something to advance the justice-related purposes she thought universities should be allowed to pursue. That was the sting of the chief justice's observation that "the serious reservations [the precedents] . . . had about racial preferences go unrecognized" in the dissents. Liberals sometimes have written about "superprecedents." For the chief justice, *Bakke* and *Grutter* were something like "inferior or subprecedents" because of the "serious reservations" they contained.

There was a cleaner route to Justice Jackson's goal. She could have said openly that *Bakke* put the law on the wrong path from the beginning. As the chief justice was happy to point out, the repeated citations in the dissenting opinions to Justice Marshall's dissent in *Bakke* did a lot to support the view that that's what the dissenters really thought.

In theory she could have said, "*Bakke* was wrong and should be ignored." Justice Jackson was foreclosed from doing that, though. Finding themselves on the defensive, the Court's liberals decided that their position on a range of issues would be strongest if they treated *stare decisis* as near-holy. *Stare decisis*, in their view, meant that later courts shouldn't ignore earlier decisions even if they thought the decisions mistaken.[3] So, for example, the *Dobbs*

---

3. I ignore as tangential to the point here some bells-and-whistles attached to the liberals' position on *stare decisis*.

decision overruling *Roe v. Wade* was wrong because it overruled *Roe,* not because *Roe* was correctly decided. It's not for me to say that their strategic judgment was mistaken. It did allow them to win some victories, as in a voting rights case decided three weeks before *SFFA,* for example. For present purposes the point is that their strategic judgment made it impossible for them to treat the Court's precedents cleanly.

The chief justice's treatment of the precedents took a classic form. Taken together the precedents established that universities could use explicit racial categories only when doing so satisfied strict scrutiny, and strict scrutiny meant that the policies had to serve a compelling interest and be narrowly tailored. But, he continued, the precedents didn't leave it at that. He extracted from them several more specific principles giving more content to those two components. Then he applied those more specific requirements to the Harvard and UNC policies, and concluded that the policies were inconsistent with what the precedents required.

All well and good so far. The problem is that if you applied those very same components—extracted, remember, from cases including *Grutter* and *Fisher* that upheld university policies—you'd have to conclude that the policies in *Grutter* and *Fisher* were unconstitutional as well. That's pretty awkward: *Grutter* upheld a policy that the principle articulated in *Grutter* tells us is unconstitutional.

We have to go through this in two steps: first, describe the more specific principles and explain why the Court concluded that the Harvard and UNC policies failed to comply with them; then apply those same principles and the reasons the Court gave in connection with Harvard and UNC to the policies upheld in *Grutter* and *Fisher.*

Drawing on some expressions of hope and expectation in *Grutter,* the chief justice wrote that *Grutter* "held" that "[a]t some point" race-based admissions programs "must end." Technically

Grutter didn't "hold" that, but transforming what *Grutter* said about end-points into a holding wasn't out of bounds. And, though the chief justice placed this "final limit" last in his list of what universities had to show, it was so central to the outcome that the next section, which applied the limits to the Harvard and UNC programs, began with the sentence, "Twenty years later, no end is in sight."

The programs had no "logical end point." How could you know when classes had "meaningful representation" of racial minorities? Only by counting the numbers until you had classes that were regularly filled with your preferred percentage of racial minorities—when you filled your quota. But, the chief justice noted, the Court had regularly rejected quotas and the associated idea of proportional representation.

The other limits flowed from strict scrutiny. As a general goal diversity was good enough. But it had to be broken down into components that were "sufficiently measurable to permit" judicial review. In management-speak, there had to be benchmarks that would allow courts to know when and how much progress toward the end point had occurred. Harvard said that it wanted to "train future leaders," "prepare graduates" to "adapt to an increasingly pluralistic society," educate students better, and "produc[e] new knowledge stemming from diverse outlooks." The chief justice responded:

> Although these are commendable goals, they are not sufficiently
> coherent for purposes of strict scrutiny. . . . [I]t is unclear how
> courts are supposed to measure any of these goals. How is a
> court to know whether leaders have been adequately "train[ed]";
> . . . or whether "new knowledge" is being developed? . . . Even
> if these goals could somehow be measured, moreover, how is
> a court to know when they have been reached, and when the
> perilous remedy of racial preferences may cease?

The chief justice supplemented this argument with another, that the admissions programs didn't "articulate a meaningful connection between the means they employ and the goals they pursue." The universities used "imprecise" racial categories to help them construct what they thought were diverse-enough classes: The category "Asian" didn't distinguish between South and East Asian applicants. And this meant, for example, that Harvard "would apparently prefer a class with 15% of students from Mexico over a class with 10% of students from several Latin American countries," but it wasn't clear why the former class would be more diverse than the latter. (To be fair to Harvard, it also wasn't clear that it would actually do that—"apparently prefer" is the giveaway.)

"The universities' main response . . . is, essentially, 'trust us.'" More formally the universities observed that *Grutter* said that the courts had "a 'tradition of giving a degree of deference to a university's academic decisions.'" But, the chief justice said, that meant only giving deference to their decision to treat the general idea of diversity as part of their mission. It didn't extend to the means they used to achieve that goal. Evaluating those means was up to the courts. "Courts may not license separating students on the basis of race without an exceedingly persuasive justification that is measurable and concrete enough to permit judicial review."

The programs were bad as well because they necessarily relied on racial stereotypes, such as the view "that there is an inherent benefit in race *qua* race," which meant (quoting UNC's lawyer), "race in itself 'says [something] about who you are.'"

Again, all well and good so far. So what did the Court say about affirmative action programs the Court had upheld—that is, about *Grutter* and *Fisher*? On the face of things you could—indeed probably would have to—say the same things about the Michigan and Texas programs that the Court said about Harvard's and UNC's—

no measurable standard or benchmarks and all that. What the chief justice did, though, was essentially wave his hands and say, "Forget about what those cases did and focus on what they said." He did this by addressing *Grutter* and *Fisher* only as they were relied upon by the dissents, asserting that the decisions didn't have to be read as holding what the dissents said they held, and indeed shouldn't be read that way.

The chief justice countered Justice Sotomayor's characterization of *Grutter* as holding that affirmative action could be used "until 'racial inequality will end,'" with "*Grutter* did no such thing." *Fisher* allowed Texas to use its program to achieve a "critical mass" of minority students but Harvard and UNC didn't rely on that justification because they didn't "even know what [the term] means." That might well be a way of saying that there's no way of measuring what a critical mass is, casting exactly the same shadow over Texas's program as the Court found for Harvard's. The chief justice's bottom line on *Grutter* and *Fisher* was that they expressed "serious reservations" about upholding affirmative action programs from Michigan and Texas. But uphold them they did, and the chief justice didn't explain why the Court shouldn't hold its nose once again and uphold what were in essence the same programs implemented in Massachusetts and North Carolina.

I can only speculate why the chief justice chose to write an opinion that dealt with the precedents so awkwardly. It did allow him to refrain from using a phrase like "*Grutter* and *Fisher* are overruled." That meant that the dissenters had to say things like, "Purporting to follow *Grutter* and *Fisher* . . ." Perhaps the chief justice was nervous about the possibility that expressly overruling those cases would trigger responses like the ones that met *Dobbs*.[4]

---

4. The cases differ, though, in that it turned out that *Roe* was quite popular (despite what the Court's conservatives might have thought) while polls even before *SFFA* showed that affirmative action isn't popular.

Writing the opinion as he did, he left it to partisans on both sides to say, "The Court effectively overruled *Grutter.*" And he made it possible for those who wanted to defend the Court as a valuable institution to say that the Court didn't go whole hog MAGA. So, for example, David French described *SFFA* as "relatively modest in scope" and said that it did "not eviscerate race-conscious remedies for documented racial discrimination." That would have been harder to say if the *SFFA* opinion expressly overruled *Grutter* and *Fisher.*

Each piece of Chief Justice Roberts's opinion is well within bounds of good judicial craft. He didn't do a good job of assembling them into an opinion that hangs together well, though.

DOCTRINE

SFFA's core argument was that race simply couldn't be considered even as part of a "holistic" overview of an applicant's file: as a shorthand, admissions officers couldn't even notice whether an applicant was white, Black, or Asian American. Justice Jackson asked SFFA's lawyer Patrick Strawbridge (who had clerked for Justice Thomas in 2008–9) an awkward question about two applicants:

> The first applicant says: I'm from North Carolina. My family has been in this area for generations, since before the Civil War, and I would like you to know that I will be the fifth generation to graduate from the University of North Carolina. I now have that opportunity to do that, and given my family background, it's important to me that I get to attend this university. I want to honor my family's legacy by going to this school.
>
> The second applicant says, I'm from North Carolina, my family's been in this area for generations, since before the Civil War, but they were slaves and never had a chance to attend this

venerable institution. As an African American, I now have that opportunity, and given my family background, it's important to me to attend this university. I want to honor my family legacy by going to this school.

. . .

The first applicant would be able to have his family background considered and valued by the institution as part of its consideration of whether or not to admit him, while the second one wouldn't be able to because his story is in many ways bound up with his race and with the race of his ancestors.

The second essay mentions the applicant's race; the first doesn't. The question was awkward because it would be weird to say that the admissions officer could take the first essay into account but not the second one.[5] You can imagine ways of saying that either both or neither could be taken into account: Statements that implicitly referred to race (the first one) had to be set aside; statements that referred to something highly correlated with race, like inability to attend UNC when it was segregated, could be considered. These and other possibilities would create problems going forward because they would either open large loopholes or generate extremely uncomfortable inquiries into exactly how admissions officers processed applications. After some fumbling, Strawbridge bit the bullet and said that the white

---

5. Justice Thomas tried to counter the "two applicants" hypothetical, which Justice Jackson incorporated into her dissent, by positing a bunch of other applicants who had, in his view, valid complaints that a Black North Carolinian was admitted while they were not. The examples are probably rhetorically effective for general readers and of course for opponents of affirmative action. They don't, however, actually address the weirdness of ignoring the Black applicant's essay while implicitly taking the white one's into account.

applicant's essay could be taken into account but not the Black applicant's.

Not surprisingly the Court's majority wasn't willing to go that far. The chief justice created his own version of the loophole Strawbridge avoided: "[N]othing in this opinion should be construed as prohibiting universities from considering an applicant's discussion of how race affected his or her life, be it through discrimination, inspiration, or otherwise." Both essays Justice Jackson described could be taken into account.

As informed readers immediately understood, this loophole could be enormous. Justice Thurgood Marshall regularly told his law clerks, "I never have to look at the back of my hand to know what race I am." His point needed no elaboration. Every experience an African American has in the United States is inflected by his or her race. At the time it wasn't central to his thinking, but I'm sure that Justice Marshall, married to a woman of Filipino descent, would have said that same thing about Asian Americans. So, every African American and Asian American could write an admissions essay connecting the student's race-related experiences, as the chief justice put it, "to *that student's* courage or determination . . . [or] *that student's* unique ability to contribute to the university. In other words, the student must be treated based on his or her experiences as an individual—not on the basis of race."

A cynic might say that the doctrine articulated by *SFFA* was simple. Universities couldn't take race "as such" into account but otherwise could take into account everything associated with race. Basically, the cynic would say, all Harvard had to do was eliminate the checkbox for "race" in admissions files, then go on as before. Justice Thomas described "a black applicant, . . . the son of a multimillionaire industrialist." The applicant could submit a personal essay describing the time he was stopped by state police while driving his father's expensive car because the police thought that a young Black man driving an expensive car had to be a drug dealer. Now he's through the loophole. All that remains is to ensure—with advice from an expensive "personal essay" coach, which his father can surely afford—that the essay is a well-written account of how race has affected his life. The cynical view does require that applicants know that they should write personal essays adverting to their race-based experiences—and that might depend upon how good their guidance counselors or other academic advisers were. Not every Black applicant might slip through the loophole but quite a few will.

The chief justice of course understood how large the loophole could be. He cautioned that "universities may not simply establish through application essays or other means the regime we hold unlawful today." And earlier in the opinion he pointed to what seems likely to be the clearest way to figure out whether universities were doing that. "For the admitted classes of 2009 through 2016 black students represented a tight band of 10.0%–11.7% of the admitted pool. The same theme held true for other minority groups." SFFA or other challengers could show that Harvard was evading the Court's decision if it turned out that, year after year, the African American proportion of the admitted class remained in that band. Challengers might not be able to win in the first year or two, but the chief justice's opinion provides a roadmap for litigation.

Again, observers saw the point right away. Elie Mystal, for example, wrote, "Colleges and universities must now punish Black applicants by decreasing the enrollment of Black students. . . . That's because the only way universities can show compliance with Roberts's new rules is to show that they've decreased the number of Black kids they let into school." Not quite. Mystal's clearly right in predicting that the easiest way to avoid immediate challenges is to cut the percentage of African Americans admitted from 10–11 percent to 7 percent—but analytically Harvard could show that it wasn't evading the Court's holding by *increasing* the percentage to 16 percent.[6]

Two other points about the chief justice's opinion. First is the "service academies" footnote. Justice O'Connor's opinion in *Grutter* had emphasized that West Point and Annapolis used affirmative action to ensure that the armed forces' officer corps would be diverse enough to be able to elicit obedience from a diverse body of enlistees. The U.S. government repeated that argument in *SFFA*. The chief justice stuck in a footnote: "No military academy is a party to these cases … [and this] opinion also does not address the issue, in light of the potentially distinct issues that military academies may present." This was of course both true and politic, but at least a bit doctrinally awkward as well. The argument that achieving diversity didn't provide enough measurable guidance to satisfy the doctrinal requirement that government interests advanced by express racial classification be compelling was central to the chief justice's argument. It's not at all clear that "get-

---

6. There's a case to be made that even preserving the 10–11 percent band over a sustained period wouldn't in itself show evasion. Harvard could point out that it was interested in ensuring diversity along a large number of dimensions. Think of it as like a museum curator trying to create an overall collection that has "enough" representation from many genres and eras and concluding that a collection ("class") with 10–11 percent African Americans, 2 percent students from the upper Midwest (the "North Dakota quota," as it's known in informed circles), 5 percent accomplished musicians, and so on down the list, is about right. So, applicants' essays describing their personal race-related experiences would be read with an eye to creating a class diverse along all these dimensions (whereas the North Dakota quota would be filled simply by looking at where the applicant came from, without reading an essay describing how being from North Dakota mattered). Of course, I would expect essentially every judge to reject this "curation" explanation, although I don't think rejection is required by the chief justice's opinion.

ting a leadership corps that matches the diversity of the enlisted troops" is any better—and it's also not clear that military leaders have any special expertise about "measurable progress" that would justify giving them but not university officials deference.

The second point is obvious. *SFFA* was about admissions, but there are a host of other programs that use affirmative action—to award scholarships, to distribute government contracts, in hiring throughout the economy, and much more. We'll find out how *SFFA* applies to such programs when the courts get and decide challenges. A case about admissions policies doesn't have to—and probably shouldn't—tell us exactly how cases about these other programs should be decided. *SFFA* provides some guidance, for example, in its requirement that there be some way to figure out when explicit racial preferences won't be justified any more, but maybe not enough—meaning that judges dealing with these follow-on challenges will often decide them based upon their predispositions rather than upon the Court's holdings.

In the end, the chief justice crafted a rather awkward doctrine—perhaps better for the headlines ("Affirmative Action Unconstitutional") than for the daily work of admissions officers.

Justice Jackson of course had an easier time of it in connection with doctrinal coherence. All she had to say was that the rules set out in *Grutter* and *Fisher* were fine and didn't need modification, much less overruling. And that's what she did.

In summary: Following the Court's prior cases didn't require Justice Jackson to formulate new doctrine. Repudiating those cases and coming up with something different (the chief justice wouldn't say "new") required a fair amount of fancy footwork. At some points—especially in creating the "experiences as an individual" loophole—the chief justice's feet got tangled up. He wouldn't be disqualified from a dance competition because of that, but it would lower his scores.

RHETORIC

Supreme Court opinions have many audiences: the litigants, of course, and people like them who need to know what they're allowed to do or barred from doing, and people in the general public who pay some attention to what the Court says, as filtered through the media sources they rely on. The justices also speak to each other through their opinions—or at least they sometimes speak *about* each other in the opinions. Good judicial craft requires that a judge choose ways of talking that communicate effectively to all these audiences.

That's no small task. The general public cares about the bottom line and the broad outlines of the reasons the justices give for their decisions; people who need to know what to do care about the nitty-gritty of the Court's doctrine. Writing an opinion that works well for both audiences is difficult. Maintaining equanimity when your colleagues disagree with you about something you think is really important is also difficult, but a well-crafted opinion will deal respectfully with the views your colleagues have and should be respectful as well of the party you're ruling against.

How well-crafted are the opinions in *SFFA*? Here I'll focus on the broad-brush arguments the justices laid out and on the ways in which they talked about each other. In brief: Chief Justice Roberts and Justices Jackson, Thomas, and Sotomayor did pretty good jobs here, although—this is clearly a matter of taste—I think that the first two did a bit better than the last two. None of them were able to sustain a respectful tone about the people they disagreed with, though—again perhaps it's a matter of taste—I think that Justice Jackson did a bit better than the chief justice and Justice Thomas.

The chief justice's opinion is *short*. Brevity lets him talk to the general audience even as it generates criticism from professionals who need doctrinal guidance. Cass Sunstein calls it "elegiac" and "almost a song." The opinion refers to "the transcendent aims" of the Fourteenth Amendment, and echoes an earlier phrase the chief justice used in saying, "Eliminating racial discrimination means eliminating all of it." He ended his opinion, "Many universities . . . have concluded, wrongly, that the touchstone of an individual's identity is not challenges bested, skills built or lessons learned but the color of their skin. Our constitutional history does not tolerate that choice." All in all, rhetorically rather effective.

Justice Jackson couldn't write as briefly because she had to lay out a more complicated analytic structure and historical account. Justices have developed a technique that allows them to combine that kind of complexity with an appeal to a general audience: Confine the latter to the opinion's opening and closing paragraphs. Justice Jackson opened her dissent, "Gulf-sized race-based gaps exist with respect to the health, wealth, and well-being of American citizens. . . . Every moment those gaps persists is a moment in which this great country falls short of actualizing one of its foundational principles—the 'self-evident' truth that all of us are created equal." Invoking the Declaration of Independence puts in relief the chief justice's reference to a "transcendent" principle in the Fourteenth Amendment. She reverts to the amendment's "promise" in describing the case's outcome as "truly a tragedy for us all." Along the way she reproduced her "two applicants" question from the oral argument and offered a robust history of how the race-based gaps she described arose from government action, not well suited for "pull quotes" but suitable for journalistic summaries. One might apply the cliché "More in sorrow than in anger" to Justice Jackson's opinion. That this is a cliché actually reflects the fact that adopting such a tone is rather rhetorically effective for the general audience.

Near the end of his brief concurrence Justice Kavanaugh wrote that "Justice Sotomayor, Justice Kagan, and Justice Jackson disagree with the Court's decision. I respect their views." Did his colleagues' opinions manifest respectful or disrespectful disagreement? Too much of the latter, I think.

Consider how the majority might have respectfully disagreed with Justice Jackson's analysis. It could point out that her analysis would support the conclusion that affirmative action could serve "remedial" purposes associated with distributive and reparative justice and that the Court's decisions from *Bakke* onward foreclosed such a justification. The chief justice wrote, "There is a reason [Justice Sotomayor's] dissent must invoke Justice Marshall's partial dissent in *Bakke* nearly a dozen times while mentioning Justice Powell's controlling opinion barely once (Justice Jackson's opinion ignores Justice Powell altogether.)" A footnote to this paragraph says expressly, "Nor has any decision of ours permitted a remedial justification for race-based college admissions." This is fair, though perhaps a bit sharper than necessary.

What does *disrespectful* critical rhetoric look like?[7] Here are examples, some triggered by the general positions taken in an opinion, others by specific statements.

- Sometimes an attempt to be colloquial conveys more disdain than an opinion should. When Justice Gorsuch described the complex rules developed to implement diversity policies as "kudzu" promoted by "bureaucrats," the image is of an invasive species deliberately introduced into the educational ecosystem. Importing a phrase from contemporary political rhetoric, Justice Sotomayor described the Court's doctrinal loophole as "an attempt to put lipstick on a pig." She added that it was "a false

7. I feel compelled to note here that Justice Scalia was well known and (in my view) mistakenly admired for his use of sharp rhetoric, such as, for example, in describing arguments made by his colleagues as "argle-bargle," or "applesauce," or one that would lead him to "hide [his] head."

promise to save face and appear attuned to reality. No one is fooled."

- Responding to the dissenters' reasonably accurate descriptions of the doctrinal loophole, the chief inserted a parenthetical phrase: "(A dissenting opinion is generally not the best source of legal advice on how to comply with the majority opinion.)" For loopholes, though, that might actually be wrong, and in any event really doesn't tell readers anything new.

- The chief justice transformed the dissenters' criticisms of the Court's displacement of decisions by democratically responsible officials into a "remarkably wrong" "false pretense of judicial humility" that allows *courts*—not university boards—to "pick[] winners and losers based on the color of their skins." This is peculiar in an opinion that expressly rejects the idea that judges should defer to university decision-makers—that is, that expressly asserts judicial power "to pick winners and losers" generally.

- Then there's the battle to claim the legacy not merely of *Brown v. Board of Education*—by now that's old hat—but to enlist the first Justice Harlan in support. Justice Jackson: "Justice Harlan knew better" in the *Civil Rights Cases* of 1883, dissenting from the Court's invalidation of a law guaranteeing equal access to public accommodations. The chief justice: "Indeed he did," quoting Harlan's dissent in *Plessy v. Ferguson;* "Our Constitution is color-blind."

- Justice Thomas described the remedial justifications implicit in Justice Jackson's dissent as "siloing us all into racial categories" and treating us as "inexorably trapped in a fundamentally racist society." Justice Jackson replied that "Justice Thomas . . . responds to a dissent I did not write" and "demonstrates an obsession with race consciousness that far outstrips my and UNC's holistic understanding." He "ignites too many straw men to list, or fully extinguish, here."

- When the tit-for-tat moves into footnotes, it's both easy to see (literally—the footnotes stand out typographically) and difficult to identify without getting too deep into the weeds. But here's one relatively simple example. Justice Jackson observed that "a higher percentage of the most academically excellent in-state Black candidates . . . were denied admission than similarly qualified White and Asian American candidates." The chief justice replied, "It is not clear how the rejection of just two black applicants over five years" showed anything significant—a reasonable invocation, perhaps, of the law of small numbers. He went on, though, to come up with what Justice Jackson then called a "back-of-the-envelope calculation" showing that "the *overall* acceptance rates of academically excellent applicants" showed "stark[]" differences. She volleyed back: "The majority's calculations of overall acceptance rates by race of *that* metric bear scant relationship to . . . how UNC's admissions process actually works (a recurring theme in its opinion)." In a footnote devoted to another battle over numbers, Justice Sotomayor wrote that the Court "misunderstands basic principles of statistics"—which seems accurate enough to caution against too heavy a reliance on *any* justice's own manipulation of data.

This list isn't complete but it's enough to suggest the psychological dynamics in which tit-for-tat responses escalate rhetorically. A judge circulates an opinion; a dissenter spots a weakness in the opinion and pokes at it; stung by the criticism, the first judge retaliates with something like "So's your old man," treating the dissent's criticisms as obviously ridiculous. (Sometimes the sequence starts with something in a proposed dissent, with the same rhetorical escalation.)

In all of these examples a justice failed to ask, "Is it really necessary for me to do this? Or at least to do it in this way?" Most times, perhaps every time, the best judges would say "No—let's let the original opinion speak for itself. I really don't need to aim some zingers at my colleagues no matter how satisfying it would be to scratch that itch."[8]

Individually the snippets I've quoted may not seem significant, and some (like Justice Gorsuch's reference to kudzu) might make an opinion more accessible to general readers. Taken together, though, they give me an uneasy sense that the Court isn't functioning well as a group of colleagues engaged in the common enterprise of devising the rules that will regulate law-making in a society where people disagree with each other.

CRAFT, RESPECTFULNESS, AND "THE MERITS"

Before wrapping up, one clarification and two qualifications about the argument for judicial craft.

The clarification: Respectfulness is a characteristic of good opinion writing, not a matter of personal relations. Good judges are respectful of the opinions voiced by their colleagues. They don't have to like each other but they should take seriously what their colleagues write—take an attitude of "charity" toward opposing arguments.[9] Justice Scalia and Justice Ginsburg were

---

8. My guess is that some sharpness is attributable to law clerks who, less mature than their bosses and without continuing ties to the other justices, may offer stronger statements than a good judge would on her own. (I drafted a dissent for Justice Marshall that said something like, "It may be easy for judges with life tenure and a salary guarantee to think" that life for poor people isn't that difficult. He sensibly enough changed it to, "It may be easy for some people to think.") If my guess about the origin of some sharpness is right, then why don't judges rein in their clerks more—why don't they tone down or eliminate overly sharp criticisms of colleagues? The answer probably has to do with dynamics within each office. I stress, though, that my guesses here are quite speculative.

9. One reader of a draft of this book pointed to a tension between my argument here and my academic reputation as something of a firebrand who has

friends, bonding in part over a shared love of opera and in part through the efforts of their spouses. Justices regularly report that they get along fine with each other in their personal interactions. We shouldn't begrudge justices (or anyone else) their friendships, of course, and it's nicer to work at a place where you get along with the people you encounter quite frequently.

Still, that has almost nothing to do with whether Justices Scalia and Ginsburg and their colleagues practiced the craft of judging well. ("Almost," because sometimes a justice will decide to refrain from publishing an opinion differing from a friend's on a minor matter—what used to be called "acquiescence" in an opinion with which you disagreed.)

The first qualification: "The merits"—whether a judge gets the answer "right" in some sense—plays almost no role in how we should assess the judge as craftsperson. Partly that's because both constitutional theory and the craft alternative assume that we're often going to disagree about what the right answer is. It's enough that some significant portion of the attentive public or some significant political elites think that the judge gets it right often enough. But that's an incredibly weak criterion. It's not beyond imagination that a judge would consistently come up with answers so "wrong" that only fervent partisans could think that the judge was actually trying to figure out what the law is or should be. More substantively, I suppose that when we look back at decisions now long in the past we might want to say that a good judge came up with what we now regard as the right answers quite a bit more often than not. That's not going to help us think

---

made more than a few disparaging comments about people with whom I disagree. I have two responses: (1) There's a difference in the academic's and the judge's roles that might justify my academic practice. (2) I was younger then and have learned from my mistakes.

about what judges do today or who we should want to put on the Supreme Court.

The second qualification, which will play a larger role in the Conclusion: The craft vision of what good judges do leaves almost no room for judges who radically disagree with the state of the law they have to work with—and in particular almost no room for judges who hold the view that the entire enterprise of judicial review is bad for the country. That shouldn't come as a surprise. What would be surprising would be a system of choosing judges that came up with such radical dissenters more than once a generation. The craft vision places bounds around what counts as good judging by drawing upon what well-socialized lawyers think good judging is.

* * *

Or maybe not. What a "good Court" is, and what "good Justices" are, are judgments made in specific historical circumstances. The grounds for such judgments change over time. Perhaps I'm simply out of date, relying on criteria that might have been appropriate in the late twentieth century when I became a law professor but have been replaced by others that I'm so unsympathetic to that I simply can't understand them. A bit more optimistically, perhaps we're experiencing challenges to previously agreed upon criteria and don't yet know whether those challenges will succeed or, as I hope, will fail.

Conclusion

I begin with two personal observations. (1) When I think about the Hughes Court and Chief Justice Hughes in particular a strong image comes to mind. I see a group of (male) leaders of the bar in some clubroom smoking their cigars and saying, "Agree or disagree with his results, you have to agree that he writes 'good' opinions." (2) In the mid-1980s I was at a conference sponsored by the American Enterprise Institute. A conservative federal judge made a joke about using the word "she" to refer to a generic judge. A few minutes later then-judge Ruth Bader Ginsburg commented in effect that she didn't think that a joking matter.

These are trivial examples but they do suggest that the assessments of the community of lawyers—about what I've called reasoned judgment or good judgment—are socially constructed. No federal judge today would make that precise joke, because the bar's composition has changed. (Today the joke might be about the practice of listing one's personal pronouns in e-mail signature blocks because the bar hasn't changed "enough.")

Here's a more significant example. In Chapter 2 I argued that good opinions were respectful of the views of those who disagreed with their results. Reflecting that sense, dissenting opinions in the Supreme Court typically though not always end with something like, "Respectfully, I dissent." I drafted an opinion for Justice Marshall in a case where he thought his colleagues were being grossly insensitive in having "fail[ed] to understand how close to the margin of survival many [poor people] are." The opinion deliberately omitted the usual closing. Justice Ginsburg, who refrained from using the phrase after around 2000, observed, "I think of my colleagues who have just criticized the court's opinion as being 'profoundly misguided' . . . [or] 'this opinion is not to be taken seriously' and then after saying that, then you end it [with 'I respectfully dissent'], . . . you've show[n] no respect at all."

Justice Antonin Scalia joined Justice Ginsburg in using the "respectfully I dissent" form much less often than his colleagues. His writing style had a conversational tone. And, as his description of his colleagues' defense of reasoned judgment as "outrageous" indicates, this style also incorporated a striking number of sharp barbs directed at his colleagues. The fact that his writing style was widely admired suggests the possibility that respectfulness is no longer required in well-crafted opinions.[1]

That possibility in turn suggests that the criteria for assessing whether a judge has good judgment can change. And here's the connection to constitutional theory: For the past few decades and perhaps longer judges threw in references to constitutional theory—originalism, the moral reading, representation-reinforcing review—either to fill the gap between their legal analysis and the results they wanted to reach, or as decoration. Perhaps, though, we're experiencing a change in the community of lawyers. Maybe more substantial references to constitutional theory, and more particularly to originalism, are becoming another characteristic of reasoned judgment. Perhaps, that is, the practice of judging is in the process of becoming more theoretical.

1. Justice Elena Kagan's style is similarly conversational but lacks the barbs. Though more than a few lower court judges have adopted Justice Scalia's practice of including "zingers" in their opinions, we'll have to wait a while to see whether it's the conversational tone alone that mattered, or whether lack of respectfulness also matters.

As I've suggested, what counts as good judging does change, but I haven't said anything about the pace of change. Chapter 1 introduced the idea of changing regimes in American political development. Those regimes seem to have had a lifespan of four or five decades. And the general story is that a regime change in the world of politics is followed, after a lag, by a regime change in the courts. Perhaps we can extend that story to the bar. After the courts change, the bar trails along.

Perhaps we're experiencing this process in real time. The widely noted and mostly decried polarization of our political life does seem to have produced a polarized Supreme Court. Put aside its substantive commitments and ask, What characterizes the Court today? Maybe the answer is, constitutional theory as a replacement for an earlier focus on judicial craft, and a sharper rhetorical style. I've read accounts of the bar in which polarization plays a role: the transformation of the American Bar Association from a bastion of professional conservatism to a liberal interest group, with a corresponding reduction in membership; the rise of the Federalist Society and, belatedly, the American Constitution Society as organizations doing what the American Bar Association used to do—generate a now-polarized understanding of what good judging entails.

I think it's a bit too early to say that the three levels of regime change that I've sketched—politics, the courts, and the bar—have taken their final shape. With that in mind, I'll end with an invocation of a more traditional sense of what good judging involves. This is what Justice Kagan had to say when introducing Chief Justice Roberts when the American Law Institute—the Establishment par excellence of the contemporary bar—gave him an award for public service:

> [Roberts has a] lawyer's mind. Not one that's prone to flights of
> fancy, but one that is grounded in and terrifically good at making

sense of legal materials. . . . His writing has deep intelligence, crystal clarity, grace, humor, and understated style. . . . His clarity, the intelligibility of his writing and his thought, his analytic precision, his ability to see and organize and make lucid whole areas of law. His ability to explain not only to lawyers but to a wider public what his decisions are based on these qualities. They're more than craft, they are the foundation stones of the rule of law. . . . They show how rules of decision are arrived at and they show how to criticize them.

Whether or not this actually describes Roberts, we can take it as a description of the kind of judge we should be looking for—today, though perhaps not for the indefinite future.

BIBLIOGRAPHIC ESSAY

CHAPTER 1

The methodological approach I take in this chapter was suggested by my reading of GAUTAM MUKUNDA, PICKING PRESIDENTS: HOW TO MAKE THE MOST CONSEQUENTIAL DECISION IN THE WORLD (2022), which is the source of the reference to the mediocrity of most presidents and justices, and the reference to brilliance. Senators Grassley and Sasse are quoted from Brian Naylor, "Barrett, an Originalist, Says Meaning of Constitution 'Doesn't Change Over Time,'" NPR, Oct. 13, 2020, available at https://www.npr.org/sections/live-amy-coney-barrett-supreme-court-confirmation/2020/10/13/923215778/barrett-an-originalist-says-meaning-of-constitution-doesn-t-change-over-time; and Lexi Lonas, "Sasse to vote no on Jackson's Supreme Court nomination," The Hill, March 25, 2022, available at https://thehill.com/homenews/senate/599841-sasse-to-vote-no-on-jacksons-supreme-court-nomination/.

Judge Posner's comments on the quality of Supreme Court justices can be found at David Lat, "Judge Richard Posner Corrects the Record Regarding His Supreme Court Comments," Above the Law, Oct. 28, 2016, available at https://abovethelaw.com/2016/10/judge-richard-posner-corrects-the-record-regarding-his-supreme-court-comments/, https://perma.cc/Y7C6-V8FV. (Justice Brennan's description of Posner is from STEPHEN B. PRESSER, LAW PROFESSORS: THREE CENTURIES OF SHAPING AMERICAN LAW 309 (2017).) Justice Owen Roberts's self-characterization can be found in MARK TUSHNET, THE OLIVER WENDELL HOLMES DEVISE HISTORY OF THE SUPREME COURT, VOL. XI, THE HUGHES COURT: FROM PROGRESSIVISM TO PLURALISM 309 (2021), where I also express some skepticism about the quotation's accuracy. In the same work I offer a qualified explanation for why the "switch in time" account is basically correct though frequently overstated.

My prediction about Justice Sotomayor's nomination is in Esquire Magazine, Oct. 7, 2008, available at https://www.esquire.com/news-politics/a5043 /sonia-sotomayor2-1008/, https://perma.cc/HG7Y-A9WB.

The lists I refer to in this chapter are Fred R. Shapiro, "Ranking the Justices," in 4 ENCYCLOPEDIA OF THE SUPREME COURT OF THE UNITED STATES 174 (David Tanenhaus ed. 2008), and Cass R. Sunstein, "Home Run Hitters of the Supreme Court," Bloomberg, Sept. 23, 2014, available at https:// www.bloomberg.com/opinion/articles/2014-04-01/home-run-hitters-of-the -supreme-court#xj4y7vzkg. Shapiro quotes William A. Ross, *The Ratings Game: Ranking Supreme Court Justices*, 79 MARQUETTE L. REV. 401, 411 (1996), on the importance of longevity. The idea of political time is developed in STE-PHEN SKOWRONEK, THE POLITICS PRESIDENTS MAKE: LEADER-SHIP FROM JOHN ADAMS TO BILL CLINTON (1997).

For material on the organization of justices' chambers, I rely on the following. Justice Powell's description of the chambers as little law firms is quoted, though without indication of the quotation's source, in IN CHAMBERS: STO-RIES OF SUPREME LAW CLERKS AND THEIR JUSTICES 391 (Todd C. Peppers & Artemus Ward eds. 2012). Justice Sotomayor asserted that it takes about five years to settle in, Justice Sonia Sotomayor in a conversation broadcast at the annual meeting of the Association of American Law Schools in January 2023, https://www.youtube.com/watch?v=WU3vFuCg92o. She and Justice Ginsburg invoke the trope of heavy editing, Sotomayor in the interview and Ginsburg in PEPPERS & WARD, at 397. Aaron Tang, *After* Dobbs: *History, Tradition, and the Uncertain Future of a Nationwide Abortion Ban*, 75 STAN. L. REV. 1091, 1128–32 (2023), explains in detail why including Alabama on the list in the Appendix to *Dobbs* was erroneous.

I developed my list of "natural courts" by searching the Supreme Court data base, http://scdb.wustl.edu/documentation.php?var=naturalCourt. The lists of potential nominees can be found at https://ballotpedia.org/Complete_list_of _Donald_Trump%27s_potential_nominees_to_the_U.S._Supreme_Court, https://perma.cc/X4JS-RWK3, and Nicholas Riccardi, "GOP Presidential Hopeful Vivek Ramaswamy Lists Senators Cruz, Lee, as Possible Supreme Court Picks," Washington Post, July 17, 2023, available at https://www.washingtonpost .com/politics/2023/07/17/ramaswamy-supreme-court-cruz-lee-ho/6e6dfc9e -24a1-11ee-9201-826e5bb78fa1_story.html.

David Danelski's analysis of the powers and roles of the chief justice, which shaped my thinking about these issues, is David J. Danelski, "The Influence of the Chief Justice in the Decisional Process of the Supreme Court Revisited," in

THE CHIEF JUSTICE: APPOINTMENT AND INFLUENCE 19 (David J. Danelski & Artemus Ward eds. 2016) (reprinting a paper originally distributed in 1960). Roberts described his hope of reducing divisions on the Court in Confirmation Hearing on the Nomination of John G. Roberts, Jr., to be Chief Justice of the United States, S. Hrg. 19-158, Serial No. J-109-37, at 303 (answer of nominee John Roberts: "I do think the Chief Justice has a particular obligation to try to achieve consensus consistent with everyone's individual oath to uphold the Constitution, and that would certainly be a priority for me if I were confirmed."). His comments on the limits of the assignment power are in John Roberts, Remarks on Receiving the Henry Friendly Award, American Law Institute, May 23, 2023, available on C-Span.org, at https://www.c-span.org/video /?528270-1/justice-kagan-chief-justice-roberts-american-law-institute -award-ceremony. Hughes and Stone as leaders at conference: WILLIAM M. WIECEK, OLIVER WENDELL HOLMES DEVISE HISTORY OF THE SUPREME COURT, VOL. XII, THE BIRTH OF THE MODERN CONSTITUTION—THE UNITED STATES SUPREME COURT, 1941–1953, at 60-62, discusses both Hughes and Stone as leaders of the Conference. Justice Brennan's comments on Chief Justice Rehnquist are from Jeffrey Rosen, "Rehnquist the Great?," The Atlantic, April 2005, available at https://www.theatlantic .com/magazine/archive/2005/04/rehnquist-the-great/303820/; Brandeis's comments on Van Devanter are quoted in MARK TUSHNET, THE OLIVER WENDELL HOLMES DEVISE HISTORY OF THE SUPREME COURT, VOL. XI, THE HUGHES COURT: FROM PROGRESSIVISM TO PLURALISM 20 (2021). SETH STERN & STEPHEN WERMIEL, JUSTICE BRENNAN: LIBERAL CHAMPION 250–53 (2010), describe Warren and Brennan as sharing the leadership role during much of the time they were on the Court together.

CHAPTER 2

The case studies in this chapter are based upon material presented in more detail and with citations in MARK TUSHNET, THE OLIVER WENDELL HOLMES DEVISE HISTORY OF THE SUPREME COURT, VOL. XI, THE HUGHES COURT: FROM PROGRESSIVISM TO PLURALISM (2021). The best discussion of the Court-packing fight is now LAURA KALMAN, FDR'S GAMBIT: THE COURT PACKING FIGHT AND THE RISE OF LEGAL LIBERALISM (2022). For the argument that pluralism requires overriding originalism, see William Baude, "Is Originalism Our Law?," 115 COLUM. L. REV. 2349 (2015).

CHAPTER 3

The argument for originalism from the oath to uphold this Constitution is offered in Evan D. Bernick & Christopher R. Green, *What Is the Object of the Constitutional Oath?*, 128 PENN STATE L. REV. 1 (2023).

Paul Brest, *The Conscientious Legislator's Guide to Constitutional Interpretation*, 27 STAN. L. REV. 585 (1975), opened scholarly discussion of constitutional interpretation by legislators. My contribution to the literature is Mark Tushnet, *Nonjudicial Review*, 40 HARV. J. LEGISLATION 455 (2003). The most systematic analysis of workarounds of which I am aware is Mark Tushnet, *Constitutional Workarounds*, 87 TEX. L. REV. 1499 (2009), though I may have missed some later work. See also Daniel A. Farber, Jonathan Gould & Matthew Stephenson, "Workarounds in American Public Law," August 29, 2023, available at https://ssrn.com/abstract=4555933, TEX. L. REV. (forthcoming). For a discussion of executive agreements as workarounds, see Curtis A. Bradley & Jack L. Goldsmith, *Presidential Control over International Law*, 131 HARV. L. REV. 1201 (2018).

JEFFREY SEGAL & HAROLD SPAETH, THE SUPREME COURT AND THE ATTITUDINAL MODEL 64 (1993), offers the canonical statement about Justices Rehnquist and Marshall. On the difficulties associated with the entire enterprise of Constitutional Theory, see J. HARVIE WILKINSON, COSMIC CONSTITUTIONAL THEORY: WHY AMERICANS ARE LOSING THEIR INALIENABLE RIGHT TO SELF-GOVERNANCE (2012). See Richard H. Fallon, Jr., "Selective Originalism and Judicial Role Morality," 102 TEX. L. REV. 221 (2023), for an examination of the practice of selective originalism, and for two early and influential articles describing the complexities associated with John Hart Ely's theory, see Mark Tushnet, *Darkness at the Edge of Town: The Contributions of John Hart Ely to Constitutional Theory*, 89 YALE L. J. 1037 (1980); Bruce A. Ackerman, *Beyond Carolene Products*, 98 HARV. L. REV. 713 (1985).

I draw on Charles Fried, *The Artificial Reason of the Law, or What Lawyers Know*, 60 TEX. L. REV. 35 (1981), for the "reasoned judgment" alternative to Constitutional Theory. For Catharine MacKinnon's skepticism about some aspects of "reasoned judgment," see Catharine A. MacKinnon, *Pornography, Civil Rights, and Speech*, 20 HARV. CIV. R.-CIV. LIB. L. REV. 1, 3 (1985).

CASS R. SUNSTEIN, HOW TO INTERPRET THE CONSTITUTION (2023), and Richard H. Fallon, Jr., *How to Choose a Constitutional Theory*, 87 CAL. L. REV. 535 (1999), discuss "choosing" constitutional theories, while Stanley Fish, *Dennis Martinez and the Uses of Theory*, 96 YALE L. J. 1773 (1987), offers in my view a better account of actual practice. (Nike adopted its slogan in 1988.

"When Did Nike Use Just Do It?," Advertising Row, Dec. 15, 2021, available at https://advertisingrow.com/advertising-magazine/when-did-nike-use-just-do-it/.) KARL LLEWELLYN, THE COMMON-LAW TRADITION: DECID-ING APPEALS 183 (1960), laid out one account of how good lawyers come to conclusions about right outcomes. I use HENRY M. HART, JR., & ALBERT M. SACKS, THE LEGAL PROCESS: BASIC PROBLEMS IN THE MAKING AND APPLICATION OF LAW 113 (William N. Eskridge, Jr., & Philip P. Frickey eds. 1994), which was widely circulated in the late 1950s but not published in book form until 1994, as my foil for raising questions about the sociological determinants of what counts at any one time and place as good lawyering.

CHAPTER 4

For examples of what Ruth Marcus calls the "cottage industry" of critiques of originalism (Ruth Marcus, "Originalism Is Bunk," https://www.washingtonpost.com/opinions/2022/12/01/originalism-liberal-lawyers-supreme-court-trap/ (originally published Dec. 1, 2022), see ERWIN CHEMERINSKY, WORSE THAN NOTHING (2022); CASS R. SUNSTEIN, HOW TO INTERPRET THE CONSTITUTION (2023). For political and intellectual histories of originalism, see JOHNATHAN O'NEILL, ORIGINALISM IN AMERICAN LAW AND POLITICS: A CONSTITUTIONAL HISTORY (2005), and ILAN WURMAN, A DEBT AGAINST THE LIVING: AN INTRODUCTION TO ORIGINALISM, ch. 1 (2017). For criticisms by academic historians of the way originalists use history, see for example JACK RAKOVE, ORIGINAL MEAN-INGS: POLITICS AND IDEAS IN THE MAKING OF THE CONSTITU-TION (1996); JONATHAN GIENAPP, THE SECOND CREATION: FIXING THE AMERICAN CONSTITUTION IN THE FOUNDING ERA (2018). The best exposition of the originalist response is William Baude & Stephen Sachs, *Originalism and the Law of the Past*, 37 L. & HIST. REV. 809 (2019), the argument of which was anticipated in Mark Tushnet, *Interdisciplinary Legal Scholarship: The Case of History-in-Law*, 71 CHI.-KENT L. REV. 909 (1996). Jefferson's letter is Jefferson to Samuel Kercheval, July 12, 1816, available at https://founders.archives.gov/?q=Ancestor%3ATSJN-03-10-02-0128&s=1511311111&r=2.

An introduction to the philosophical literature on shared agency is Abraham Sesshu Roth, "Shared Agency," The Stanford Encyclopedia of Philosophy (Summer 2017 Edition), Edward N. Zalta (ed.), available at https://plato.stanford.edu/archives/sum2017/entries/shared-agency/.

For the move away from the due process clause to the "privileges or immunities" clause see CHRISTOPHER R. GREEN, EQUAL CITIZENSHIP,

CIVIL RIGHTS, AND THE CONSTITUTION: THE ORIGINAL SENSE OF THE PRIVILEGES OR IMMUNITIES CLAUSE (2015); ILAN WURMAN, THE SECOND FOUNDING: AN INTRODUCTION TO THE FOURTEENTH AMENDMENT (2020). McConnell's article on *Brown* is Michael W. McConnell, *Originalism and the Desegregation Decisions,* 81 VA. L. REV. 947 (1995).

The opinions used to illustrate the similarity between living constitutionalism and "abstract meaning" originalism are Harper v. Virginia Board of Elections, 383 U.S. 663, 669 (1966), Citizens United v. FEC, 558 U.S. 310 (2010), and United States v. Stevens, 559 U.S. 460 (2010).

The most important works on the ideas of liquidation and of the "construction zone" are William Baude, *Constitutional Liquidation,* 71 STAN. L. REV. 1 (2019), and KEITH E. WHITINGTON, CONSTITUTIONAL CONSTRUCTION: DIVIDED POWERS AND CONSTITUTIONAL MEANING (1999); Lawrence B. Solum, *Originalism and Constitutional Construction,* 82 Fordham L. Rev. 453 (2013). The illustrations I rely on come from Randy E. Barnett, *New Evidence of the Original Meaning of the Commerce Clause,* 55 ARK. L. REV. 847 (2003), and a list in Justice Gorsuch's concurring opinion in West Virginia v. EPA, 142 S. Ct. 2587, 2625 n. 6 (2022). For liberals "catching on," see, for example, Jack Balkin, *Commerce,* 109 MICH. L. REV. 1 (2010); Julian Davis Mortensen & Nicholas Bagley, *Delegation at the Founding,* 121 COLUM. L. REV. 277 (2021); Nicholas R. Parillo, *A Critical Assessment of the Originalist Case Against Administrative Regulatory Power: New Evidence from the Federal Tax on Private Real Estate in the 1790s,* 130 YALE L. J. 1288 (2021).

Recent developments in originalism include the "preponderance of evidence" approach in John O. McGinnis & Michael B. Rappaport, *The Power of Interpretation: Minimizing the Construction Zone,* 96 NOTRE DAME L. REV. 919 (2021) (describing a "51–49" rule). For corpus linguistics, see Kevin Tobia, "The Corpus and the Courts," https://lawreviewblog.uchicago.edu/2021/03/05 /tobia-corpus/, a substantial essay responding to Thomas R. Lee & Stephen Mouritsen, *The Corpus and the Critics,* 88 U. CHI. L. REV. 275 (2021), the "two moderate enthusiasts" referred to. (For "amicus wrangling" see Allison Orr Larsen & Neal Devins, *The Amicus Machine,* 102 VA. L. REV. 1901 (2016)). The case study of corpus linguistics and the Second Amendment relies on Josh Blackman & James C. Phillips, "Corpus Linguistics and the Second Amendment," Aug. 7, 2018, https://blog.harvardlawreview.org/corpus-linguistics-and -the-second-amendment/, updated in James Cleith Phillips & Josh Blackman, *Corpus Linguistics and Heller,* 56 WAKE FOREST L. REV. 609 (2021), and Brief for Corpus Linguistics Professors and Experts as Amici Curiae Supporting Respondents, New York State Rifle & Pistol Ass'n v. City of New York, No. 18-280, Aug. 12, 2019. I refer to two prominent originalists' responses to erroneous decisions, William Baude & Stephen Sachs, *Originalism's Bite*, 20 GREEN BAG 2ND 103 (2016).

CHAPTER 5

JEREMY WALDRON, LAW AND DISAGREEMENT (1999), is the major presentation of arguments for the proposition that non-judges can be constitutionally responsible. (My qualification about intentional action against despised minorities is developed in Mark Tushnet, Trump v. Hawaii: *"This President" and the National Security Constitution*, 2018 SUPREME COURT REV. 1, in connection with Chief Justice Roberts's opinion in Trump v. Hawaii, 138 S. Ct. 2392 (2018).)

James Bradley Thayer, *The Origin and Scope of the American Doctrine of Constitutional Law*, 7 HARV. L. REV. 129 (1893), remains central to thinking about alternatives to Constitutional Theory. (For a fascinating presentation of crazy constitutional interpretations, see JARED A. GOLDSTEIN, REAL AMERICANS: NATIONAL IDENTITY, VIOLENCE, AND THE CONSTITUTION (2022).) Sunstein's updating of Thayer "minimalism" is CASS R. SUNSTEIN, ONE CASE AT A TIME: JUDICIAL MINIMALISM ON THE SUPREME COURT (2002). The argument that Chief Justice Roberts is sometimes a minimalist is offered in, for example, "Chief Justice Says His Goal Is More Consensus on Court," New York Times, May 22, 2006, available at https://www.nytimes.com/2006/05/22/washington/22justice.html.

My "intellectual history" of the "takes a theory" aphorism draws on Lawrence Solum, "Legal Theory Lexicon: It Takes a Theory to Beat a Theory," available at https://lsolum.typepad.com/legaltheory/2022/02/legal-theory-lexicon-it-takes-a-theory-to-beat-a-theory.html. The key works that shaped my understanding of theory change in the natural sciences are THOMAS KUHN, THE STRUCTURE OF SCIENTIFIC REVOLUTIONS (1962); N.R. HANSON, PATTERNS OF DISCOVERY (1958); and PETER GALLISON, HOW EXPERIMENTS END (1987). Probably the most famous example of the influence of theoretical presuppositions on the assessment of empirical evidence in physics is the way in which physicists seeking to confirm Einstein's theory of relativity interpreted various ambiguous and inconsistent observations of the displacement of observations of Mercury by the sun's gravity. A good and balanced account is DANIEL KENNEFICK, NO SHADOW OF A DOUBT: THE 1919

ECLIPSE THAT CONFIRMED EINSTEIN'S THEORY OF RELATIVITY
(2019).

Defenses of pluralism are PHILIP BOBBITT, CONSTITUTIONAL
FATE: THEORY OF THE CONSTITUTION (1982); PHILIP BOBBITT,
CONSTITUTIONAL INTERPRETATION (1991); and RICHARD H. FAL-
LON, JR., IMPLEMENTING THE CONSTITUTION (2001). (I draw the
statistics on the percentage of women lawyers in 1940 from J. Gordon Hylton,
"Adam's Rib as an Historical Document: The Plight of Women Lawyers in the
1940s," Marquette University Faculty Blog, June 4, 2013, available at https://law
.marquette.edu/facultyblog/2013/06/adams-rib-as-historical-document/, https://
perma.cc/Q45Y-C7X3.)

CHAPTER 6

For Justice Jackson's question at oral argument see Transcript of Oral Argument,
SFFA v. University of North Carolina, No. 21-70, Oct. 21, 2022, pp. 65–66, available at https://www.supremecourt.gov/oral_arguments/argument_transcript
/2022. Mark Graber's reference to the Oakland Athletics is in Mark Graber,
"'History' and History in Students for Fair Admission," Balkinization, June 30,
2023, available at https://balkin.blogspot.com/2023/06/history-and-history-in
-students-for.html; and Michael's Dorf's reference to the "pesky" word *invidious*
is at Michael Dorf, "Precedents Out of Context in the Harvard/UNC Affirmative Action Ruling," Dorf on Law, June 29, 2023, available at https://www.dorfon
law.org/2023/06/precedents-out-of-context-in-harvardunc.html.

Elie Mystal, "The White Media Has Missed a Key Part of the Affirmative
Action Ruling," The Nation, July 12, 2023, available at https://www.thenation
.com/article/society/what-the-media-is-missing-about-the-supreme-courts
-affirmative-action-ruling/, makes the now widely understood point about the
loophole in *SFFA*, though he identifies only the downside pressure and not the
upside possibilities. The "shantytown" law review article that Justice Thomas
cited is Michael Rappaport, *Originalism and the Colorblind Constitution*, 89
NOTRE DAME L. REV. 71 (2013). David French's assessment of the decision is
David French, "I Don't See a 'Rogue' Supreme Court," New York Times, Aug. 4,
2023, available at https://www.nytimes.com/2023/08/04/opinion/sunday/supreme
-court-conservative.html.

The restorative justice argument for affirmative action is made implicitly in
"President Lyndon Johnson's Commencement Address at Howard University,"
June 4, 1965, available at https://dwkcommentaries.com/2020/02/26/president
-lyndon-johnsons-commencement-address-at-howard-university/. The voting

rights victory that made it awkward to assert that *Bakke* was wrong is Allen v. Milligan, 143 S. Ct. 1487 (2023).

A good presentation of the argument for the importance of charity toward one's judicial colleagues is Thomas C. Donnelly, *Supreme Court Legitimacy: A Turn to Constitutional Practice*, 47 BYU L. REV. 1487, 1517–21 (2022). Examples of Justice Scalia's quotable but non-charitable phrases are "argle-bargle" in United States v. Windsor, 570 U.S. 744 (2013); "applesauce" in King v. Burwell, 576 U.S. 473 (2015); "hide my head" in Obergefell v. Hodges, 576 U.S. 644 (2015).

CONCLUSION

The Marshall opinion referred to is United States v. Kras, 409 U.S. 434 (1973). Justice Ginsburg's comment on the phrase "respectfully dissent" is found in Ryan Teague Beckwith, "The Two Harshest Words Antonin Scalia Used Against Obamacare," Time Magazine, June 25, 2015, available at https://time.com /3935812/supreme-court-antonin-scalia-dissent/, https://perma.cc/SL6D-MQ8H. Justice Scalia's comment on the phrase can be found in Note, *From Consensus to Collegiality: The Origin of the 'Respectful' Dissent*, 124 HARV. L. REV. 1305 (2011), which also has a valuable examination of the phrase's history. Justice Kagan's description of Chief Justice Roberts is from her Address to American Law Institute, May 23, 2023, awarding John Roberts the Henry Friendly Medal, available at https://www.c-span.org/video/?528270-1/justice-kagan-chief-justice -roberts-american-law-institute-award-ceremony.

INDEX

Index

Index

Index